HOPE DEALERS

The Calling, The Struggles,
The Breakthroughs, and
The Community of Believers

NADINE BLASE PSAREAS

ISBN: 978-1-733-0023-0-1 (ebook)

Cover Design: Tess Helmandollar/ The Cognitive Creative

Graphic Design: AYGD Graphic Design/ Angela Yadid

Interior Book Layout: Jen Henderson/ Wild Words Formatting

Promo Video Producer: Edge of the Frame, LLC/ Patrick James Thomas

Website Design: Marcellinus Okeke/ 2 Logics

Publishing and Coaching: Gary Williams/ Chandler Bolt's Self-Publishing School

Developmental Editor: Silverman Editing/ Laura Silverman

Marketing and Promotion: Laura Peterson

Line Editor and Proofreader: Flora Brown

WHAT OTHERS ARE SAYING ABOUT NADINE BLASE PSAREAS AND *HOPE DEALERS*

"*HOPE DEALERS* is more than just another book... it is a global movement of hope to those who've grown weary in the struggles of life. Nadine leads the charge offering you insight and inspiration to never give up."

Rudy Ruettiger
Inspiration behind the movie RUDY and Motivational Speaker

"*HOPE DEALERS* connects with people going through many different struggles, yet all in the same powerful way. Nadine's commitment to personal growth and development over the years is evidenced through the different victories she shares. This book will help equip and empower you to never quit when obstacles enter your life. This is a perfect read for those needing an inspirational push and insight knowing that the only way through is through and that joy awaits on the other side."

Jefferson Santos
Speaker, International Trainer,
and #1 Best Selling Author of *Higher Life Design*
@JeffersonFsantos

"True wealth and peace reside in a person's story, telling it in a way that motivates and uplifts others to reach their highest potential. Nadine's journey of hope and faith will challenge any reader to overcome the impossible and live life to its fullest.

Kim Ha Campbell
International Best Selling Author of *Inner Peace Outer Abundance*,
Real Estate Expansion Expert, Speaker

"Page after page, *HOPE DEALERS* challenges you, celebrates you, and invites you to unlock your life for unlimited and unprecedented abundance! Nadine has not only curated an extraordinary book, she's created the opportunity for you to challenge the limits of what you believe is possible for yourself and she invites you to unleash your gifts so that you can, in turn, give hope to others."

Davide Di Giorgio
Speaker, Ambassador,
and #1 International Best Selling Author of *Being Unapologetic*

"This is a must read! Nadine shares what she's learned on the front lines of an extraordinary personal and business life. She offers you the inspiration to pursue personal development that assists you with insight as you journey through the struggles only to find the joy in the breakthrough was worth it all. Nadine is the leader that will guide you to make an impact and inspire others."

Del Hughes
Non-Profit Founder of Atlanta Volleyball Institute
provided college scholarships to 264 young ladies,
7 International Championship and National Champions

DOWNLOAD THE E-BOOK FREE!

READ THIS FIRST

Just to say thanks for buying my book,
I would like to give you the E-book version 100% FREE!

Go to: http://hopedealersbookpdf.com

DEDICATION

This book is dedicated to the following people:

My husband
Peter Psareas
Without his love and support, there would be no book,
no nonprofit, and certainly fewer adventures.

My son
Nick Porter
Without his journey, there would be no nonprofit created
in the first place, resulting in fewer people ever receiving help.

My parents
Nick and Dianne Blase
I am grateful for the foundational faith and values they've laid for me.
Without that example, I would not be who I am today.

My grandma
Mrs. Margaret Mary Blase
Grandma always gave to us limitlessly. She loved us unconditionally. She poured
her heart and soul into us. Here is my gift back to her. She would be proud of me.

My God
Most importantly, I dedicate this book to Jehovah God.
This book is a testimony of your work. Use as you will. All of it is for you.

In the end, I just want to hear God speak these words to me, "Well done, good and faithful
servant; you gave it your best shot, and you trusted in me. In spite of your imperfect
humanity, you are acceptable, pleasing, and perfect in my sight."

QUOTES

"The Opposite of Addiction is Connection."
—Johann Hari

"When you are going through hell, don't stop and pitch a tent."
—Jefferson Santos

"The only way through is through."
—Wayne Nugent

"Strive to assume the best in others, always giving others the benefit of the doubt."
—Josh Paine

"Who you surround yourself with is who you become."
—Jim Rohn

"The past does not determine your future."
—Johnny Wimbrey

"Your talent is God's gift to you. What you do with it is your gift back to God."
—Leo Buscaglia

"If you don't find a way to make money while you sleep, you will work till the day you die."
—Warren Buffett

"Change your friends or change your friends."
—Dave Ulloa

"Show me your friends and I'll show you your future."
—Mark Ambrose

"Bad things happen; how I respond to them defines my character and the quality of my life. I can choose to sit in perpetual sadness, immobilized by the gravity of my loss, or I can choose to rise from the pain and treasure the most precious gift I have—life itself."
—Walter Anderson

"Everything that happens was meant to happen, there's a purpose for everything."
—Aunt Margaret Blase Cohen

"Embrace and accept all of your past, the good and the bad, learn from it, and realize its intent that molds you into a greater person."
—Sylina "Two Bears"

"Be the change that you want to see in the world."
—Mahatma Gandhi

"A man is but a product of his thoughts. What he thinks he becomes."
—Napolean Hill/Gandhi

"If you want what the average person doesn't have, then you've got to do what the average person won't do."
—Jeff Bolf

"Do not be conformed to the things of this world, but be transformed by the renewing of your mind."
—Romans 12:2

CONTENTS

INTRODUCTION

Hope is gravely and dangerously deficient in our world today. Struggles occur with relationships, marriages, addictions, businesses, finances, health, weight loss, emotions, mental wellness, grief and loss, and spirituality. All these challenges scream for just a glimpse of hope to make life worthwhile and to give ourselves meaning and purpose. People have become suicidal, homicidal, and passively destructive without even realizing. Apathetic, lonely in relationships, disconnected, purposeless, sick, unhealthy, overweight, addicted to all sorts of different things, not just substances. People have become outright confused as to what is the purpose or meaning in life at all. They've come to their wit's end, the depths of despair, and the definition of hopelessness. Some in just one or two areas of life, and many in multiple areas.

For some, the word hope produces immediate feelings of disappointment, failure, pipe dreams, and even danger. For the parent, the spouse, the addict, or the entrepreneur, the idea of hope can be frightening. Why? Because if they invest their faith in hope, it can be the path to pipe dreams, too good to be true, failure, disappointments, reality, and let downs. For the prisoner, hope can be downright dangerous.

This book restores hope in its rightful place. It ushers in hope and inspiration to those who have been imprisoned in their minds and their lives for much too long. Through the collections of real-life stories, experiences, and the resources given, you will inhale a much-needed breath of fresh air. You will find the inspiration and motivation to have faith and hope again. You'll discover the value of connection to others and the realization of knowing you are never alone.

In my early 40s, I found myself to be a newly successful entrepreneur, and simultaneously, the mother of a heroin addict. This plunged me into an unexpected journey I could have never imagined. On my quest to find hope, I discovered powerfully liberating lessons.

Within the pages of this book, I invite you to experience unique perspectives. Through this lens of hope, I've come to recognize challenges as opportunities. I've come to view circumstances and learn that things don't happen *to* me, things happen *for* me. Then, as I dove one level deeper, I discovered that things started happening *through* me. I've recognized that everything happens for a reason, things were actually meant to happen, and everything has its purpose.

You will come to find your hope that was once lost, even if it's just in one area of your life, through the personal stories as I reveal the realization of my calling, finding hope and peace in the midst of the struggle, collecting smiles through the breakthroughs, and unifying together with others to serve one mission . . . and that is to deal *hope*. Your heart will be touched in unexpected ways, and you will take the risk to reclaim hope again. There will be at least one part, if not many parts of this book that will inspire you to discover, find, and experience hope again. I promise there is hope for the afflicted and those who are in despair. There's healing for the broken-hearted, there is freedom for those who are captive, and there is the release from darkness and the opening of the eyes for all who have been imprisoned. There is fun, freedom, and fulfillment to be discovered, lived, and mastered.

Don't be that person who remains close-minded and misses out on opportunities because you have temporarily lost faith and hope. Be the kind of person who turns their tests into testimonies, learn to be the kind of person who turns their mess into messages; be that person who reclaims their beauty from ashes. ***This is your life!***

This book is structured in ways for you to choose what applies to you so that you can maximize your time. There are several different sections. It is not necessary for you to read every section.

Lastly, many parts of this book share several personal experiences that are deeply founded on my personal faith. I want to offer a spiritual disclaimer: These personal experiences are not meant to persuade or convince you of any particular religious belief, but they are simply me sharing how my experiences played out.

The hope you are about to read about will inspire you to look at life in a way that you never thought possible, or perhaps were unwilling to take the risk. You will gain an awareness that leads to a life-altering pathway to freedom. You will feel connected again, and you will not ever look back to hopelessness and despair again.

You will begin to find joy and breakthroughs as you discover the power of using your own story to bring hope to others.

The Conception and The Calling

CHAPTER 1

The Name

I've come to discover over the years how the pieces of my life puzzle have started coming together. I am far from the puzzle being completed, but I can definitely see the border pieces taking a framed shape. There are still so many pieces continuing to come together on the interior, and that's the journey that keeps going until the day I leave this earth, and hopefully after that as I intend to leave a legacy.

I remember my Aunt Margaret telling me, after going through my first divorce, that everything happens for a reason, and everything has its purpose. That awareness became life-altering for me, and it began my journey and pathway to freedom.

Looking back into my earlier years, I think about the simple act in which my mother named me. When looking up the origin of my name, I discovered that Nadine means hope. Just one word, hope. This derivative is found in Slavic, French, Russian, and Greek translations. One word . . . hope. I'm not sure that my mother intended to name me Hope. In fact, she told me she named me after a beautiful young student in her French class. I actually think my mother had no clue about what she was really naming me, nor was she aware of the lifelong implications it would have on me. I'm certain God had something to do with placing that name in my mother's heart, unbeknownst to her at the time. So it was, and so it came to be. Ever since I can remember as a child, I've always had this unexplainable hope and faith towards situations and circumstances, that I came to realize later was not typical.

Nadine

Local Origin of Name: English
From the Russian name Nadia

Meaning
'Hope'

Nadine
One who is full of hope....

Nadine
It has a Slavic origin, and its meaning
is "hope". Variant of Nadia.

Nadine
Meaning: Hope
Origin: French, Russian

CHAPTER 2

Marcy State, Miss Grace, and Yankee Stadium

Around the age of 8 years old, I recall visiting Marcy State Hospital, a former psychiatric hospital in Upstate NY for people of all ages who at that time were labeled "mentally retarded." We went there as a group from the church as a community outreach project over the holidays. We would sing Christmas songs to their residents. It made me so happy to bring hope to those who were less fortunate. When I saw them smile, it made me smile, and everyone who observed also smiled. That was my first experience, I can recall, of a "hope deal." The feeling I got from that "transaction" was addictive. I had to have more. Just to be clear, a "hope deal" is defined as the transaction from one person dealing hope to another. I went on to experience more outreach projects in nursing homes with my father and his church. I loved visiting with the elderly, singing songs, listening to them speak, and giving them much desired company to help shine over their loneliness.

Then, later on, the hopedealing seemed to carry on into my college years, at the University of Georgia with my best friend, Meredith. We found ourselves at the nursing home on Baxter Street, going in, reading, and visiting with the residents there. We absolutely got our "hope fix" by bringing joy and hope to others who were starving for some interaction. We just loved to deliver/deal hope! I recall one older woman, named Grace, that I connected with. I'd visit her regularly. She always loved and wanted me to open her Bible for her and read and read and read to her. She'd smile so big, and so would I. Connecting with others felt great!

That's when I learned about delivering hope, or maybe that was the start of the early days of dealing hope. It's never about me getting recognition or being some heroic saint for investing in those less fortunate. Honestly, I would start going into each situation thinking that I was delivering a blessing and that I was the giver of the blessing, only to find out the opposite. By the time I was done with the entire transaction, my heart was so warmed and fulfilled that I ended up being the one receiving the blessing. It was pretty cool to see how all that worked out. One day, I remember walking into the nursing home in Athens to visit Miss Grace, only to find that her bed was empty; she had gone home to heaven that she always spoke about to me. I was so grateful at that moment for the time I had gotten to spend with my precious friend in her last days. I could never put a price on that experience.

My parents brought me up in an atmosphere that always seemed to promote a charitable lifestyle. I'm so grateful for the example my parents role-modeled for me, and never to overlook those less fortunate. I remember my dad always, to this day, giving in some way or another to those less fortunate. My mother, on the other hand, being the typical Italian mother that she still is, would always cook for others. They are always giving giving giving food food food. Even to this day, to see my adult boys' eyes light up when Grammi puts one of her famous homemade sausage breads in their hands to take to their own respective homes.

One time, I remember going with my father and my cousin to a New York Yankees game down in the city at Yankee Stadium. The Yankees were, of course, our *favorite* and the ***best*** team that ever existed on the face of this earth, right dad? My cousin, Victor Colenzo, was terminally ill suffering from cerebral palsy. It was no easy task to take a severely disabled young man in a wheelchair to travel into the city to a major sporting event or anywhere for that matter. However, my dad wanted to make sure that Victor had this incredible experience before his illness grew much worse. There we were again . . . being the "givers of the blessing" only to find that we were the recipients in the end when . . . holy cow . . . because my cousin was terminal, we got to meet Lou Piniella and Reggie Jackson! What a memory I will never forget! All this centered on dealing hope.

CHAPTER 3

Cujo and the Angel

For my very first job, I was the neighborhood newspaper delivery girl for the Observer Dispatch in our small town of New Hartford, just outside of Utica, in upstate NY. Me and my 10-speed bicycle and a bag containing carefully rolled up newspapers slung sideways across my chest zipped around that block generating a whopping $100 a month, which I thought was pretty good for an 11-year-old blooming entrepreneur.

There was this one house towards the end of my route that had a very large, angry, scary dog on a questionable chain tied to a stake that ferociously barked at me every time I delivered their newspaper. Each time, I would anxiously throw the paper into the yard and phew . . . speed off feeling like I had narrowly escaped death from the jaws of hell tearing me apart. Wow, I learned early on that entrepreneurship does not come without risks, yet the juice is always worth the squeeze. Back then, at the turn of 1980, I can tell you I was the most successful 11-year-old 6th grader amongst my peers with $100 a month earnings in my pocket.

One day, as I passed "Cujo's" house, I noticed a premature ceasing of the ferocious barking. As I turned around, to my horror, Cujo broke his chain and was running full force towards an early meat dinner . . . ME! I knew then I was a goner. Powered by this massive rush of adrenaline, I broke record speed on my bicycle wildly and frantically racing into what was a field in front of my elementary school across the street from my house on Higby Rd. I lost control of my bike. The perfectly rolled newspapers in the bag were flying in every direction in the air. My bike slung over to the other direction, and behind me . . . "Cujo" . . . behind me running with eyes bugging out in hopes of devouring his long-awaited Italian meal. Suddenly, as I picked my head up and looked forward, a brown car appeared in the middle of the field out of nowhere. A lady leaned over to the passenger side yelling out the window, "Hurry, hurry, get in!" All those lessons about getting in the car with strangers had no significance in my life at that given moment. I got up and flung myself in her car and slammed the door just in time before old Cujo could even get a nip at my toe.

She drove me directly across the field onto the street and into the driveway of my green house. I thanked her and ran out of the car breathless to go tell mom and dad what happened. They came running outside to see that no car was there. She was gone! They made me describe the car and the driver inside. It was a small town, almost everyone knew each other. But no one had heard of the description of this lady with this brown car. My parents were just thankful I was alive. So was I. As my father was walking up the street with a baseball bat in his right hand ready to have an Italian conversation with Cujo's owners, my mother stayed with me in the house and comforted me in my moment of post-trauma with some pepperoni and mozzarella.

I went to bed that night, knowing without a shadow of a doubt that I had a supernatural encounter with an angel. I believed in God at that moment and knew He sent his angel to protect me. Ever since that experience, hope was ignited in me, as I believed without a shadow of a doubt that God had his hand on me and had a special purpose and mission for my life. I've never once doubted God's provision, protection, or promises for me since that day. Hope, faith, and belief were solidified in my heart. I sang little songs to God and chanted my little homemade prayers to Him every night when I'd go to bed for years after that. I also began to consider that perhaps the supernatural realm was much more real than reality itself. This was the first of a few other supernatural encounters that I would experience later in life that constructed hope.

CHAPTER 4

The College Days: Camp Calvin and the Jungles of Haiti

One summer, when I was in school at the University of Georgia, I faced the decision of what to accomplish during my summer break. Meredith and I decided that instead of vacationing to exotic destinations like most of our classmates seemed to do, we decided to serve as camp counselors at Camp Calvin in Hampton, GA. To my surprise, I was assigned to a cabin of children diagnosed with ADHD, a fairly new term back then in 1990. Yikes! Were they going to scare me away? I wondered. However, my love for serving children who had challenges began to grow as I was determined to find the beauty and strength in each one, in spite of what others found to be problematic with them.

As I was just getting comfortable with the daily routine, a rainy day occurred at Camp Calvin! I had a cabin full of ADHD 9-year-old kids! Our sunshiny weather plans were destroyed. Well, hope was not lost! We ended up putting on our swimsuits and shorts and created a new activity called mud puddle hopping. We found every mud puddle we could on that property and splashed belly first in each puddle covering ourselves in mud like the happiest piggies on the face of this earth. We giggled so hard for hours that our bellies began to hurt! What fun! Hopelessness can be both small scale and large scale—yes, it's important to help save lives, but on a small scale, it's also important to transform a rainy-day into fun if you can! When hope was nowhere to be found, we just had to create our own hope!

```
the Lord said go →(TO CAMP CALVIN)
and i said who me
and He said yes, you
and i said
"but i'm not ready yet
and an important meeting is coming up
and i can't leave my work right now
and you know there is no one to take my place"
and He said "you're stalling"

        again the Lord said go
        and i said but i don't want to
        and He said "I didn't ask if you wanted to"
        and i said
        "listen, i'm not the kind of person
        to get involved in controversy
        besides my family won't like it
        and what will my neighbors think"
        and He said "baloney"

and yet a third time the Lord said go
and i said "do i have to?"
and He said "do you love me?"
and i said
"look i'm scared
people are going to hate me
and cut me up into little pieces
i can't take it all by myself "
and He said "where do you think I'll be?"

        and the Lord said go
        and i sighed
        "here i am, send me."

                --the Rev. George F. Tittman
```

As the next summer break approached, I decided to travel a little farther south and experience a mission trip in Haiti. It was 2 weeks before a military coup broke out and tension was rising in Port au Prince. Along with serving in an orphanage, we also proceeded to set up a medical station in which we dispensed medicine and supplies that we had smuggled into the country to distribute. I remember craftily sewing meds into the lining of our suitcases in order to pass through customs. I recall learning how to administer a shot by practicing on oranges. I remember very thin children having bellies the size of a basketball. We would give them this medicine supposedly derived from green peppers that would make them expel the parasites out of their swollen bellies.

I recall the grueling 8-hour drive traveling out into the jungle and villages in the mountains. No bathrooms existed anywhere. We had to locate a bush or an outhouse with a hole in the ground to relieve ourselves. I remember one time we were in a jungle village where we had heard that no white man had ever been before. I had to pee. I sprinted to a bush to empty my bladder. When I glanced up, there was a large group of children glaring at me. Some were giggling, some with jaws dropped, and I assume because they had never seen so much white skin in their lives! I remember sleeping on dirt floors in the family's homes who welcomed us. I also recall hearing the yelps in the distance of the voodoo animal sacrifices. There was also a pregnant woman with severe burns coming to our medical station set up in the village that day. We discovered that a voodoo witch doctor was chanting over her when a lantern blew up and burned her from head to toe.

When we finally left the village, we brought 2 very ill babies with us. The malnourishment, dehydration, AIDs, and many other diseases were so rampant in the mountains and jungles of Haiti. It was devastating. The women kept having children with no education about health or disease. Sadly, they unknowingly kept giving birth to one HIV infected child after another. I'll never forget taking turns with my friends holding these babies the entire 8-hour drive back to the orphanage. Unfortunately, both babies had died by the time we arrived back to Port au Prince. Our hearts were so heavy, and we remained speechless to one another. One baby died in my own arms as we sang soft sweet loving words to them. It was one of the most eye-opening sobering experiences I've ever had in my life.

It was life-changing to have had the opportunity at that young age of 19 to deliver hope in a severely oppressed community through dispensing medicine, sharing our faith, interacting, and connecting with the people there. I developed a tremendous appreciation for our conveniences and quality of life in the USA, as this was evidenced upon arriving back home into the Miami airport. I ran directly to the restroom, got on my knees, embraced and kissed the porcelain toilet with a level of gratitude I never had prior.

That mission trip impacted me so much that I returned to the University of Georgia and changed my major. I had entered UGA as an accounting major in Terry College of Business; however, I ended up graduating from Aderhold College of Education with a bachelor's degree in education. I figured dealing hope to children as a school teacher would be more rewarding than filing people's taxes as a CPA. Not once did I even consider the financial aspect of those careers. I simply followed my heart.

While on the Haiti mission trip, I had met Scott. We continued our relationship as I returned to school. Nine months later, we were married. In the middle of all my college education at UGA, I found myself married, and then within 2 years after that, I found myself with 2 cute adorable little boys. Thank God I was in the field of "child education and development." Being in that field allowed me the grace to bring my two little boys into my classes with me. At that point in my last year of school with 2 young children, I was so financially challenged. I could not even afford a single textbook for any of my classes. I decided to attend every single class and take impeccable notes hoping I could make it without the required materials. I ended up with straight A's and made the Dean's List, with no textbooks, a small rambunctious toddler on one knee, and a baby on the other. I was determined to make magic happen and find hope in the situation in spite of not having the finances I needed to purchase textbooks.

CHAPTER 5

The Scientific Process
of the Hope Transaction

More recently, I had a dear friend and colleague, Kit Cummings, scientifically dissect and explain this entire amazing process that occurs in the body with dopamine. It was the unveiling and enlightenment of such a simple concept . . . revealed in a whole new light.

Kit is an international motivational speaker, best-selling author, and the founder of an amazing 501c3 nonprofit organization called the Power of Peace Productions and the Power of Peace Project. Hope is the New Dope is his registered slogan he is well known for creating. He goes further to validate this slogan by explaining the dopamine transaction that occurs in the human body.

As a recovered alcoholic, he found that the magic behind a life of sobriety was to participate in this dopamine transaction acquired by serving others. This actually became a new addiction for him, validating that Hope *is* the New Dope. When you simply say something encouraging to another, do something kind to another, serve another, perform an act of love for another, and you put a smile on their faces or make them feel good, then biochemically in their body, ***dopamine is increased***. That's cool. However, the cooler part is when the person ***doing the dealing*** sees the smile on the recipient's face; now their dopamine is increased (that's the addicting part). Then, here's where it gets even crazier; if anyone else is around observing this whole transaction, *they too* experience an increase in dopamine in their body—just from witnessing the whole deal. Next thing you know, you've got dopamine flinging around all over the place like a virus hitting up everyone present. Now you have a big huge Hope is the New Dopefest! Simple, powerful, and addicting! This is the type of dopamine we were created for experiencing; the natural God-given high we were intended to enjoy. Sadly, many people are unsuccessful with this process of connecting with one another which can result in a dopamine deficiency. Many have come to lose hope and often turn to substances or other addictive behaviors to satisfy their dopamine craving in synthetic ways that can lead to severe illness and death.

CHAPTER 6

Why am I Writing this Book???

I want to inspire others to discover, find, and experience their own hope. Then, I want to be able to equip others to deal hope. My intent is not to push any religious or philosophical belief upon anyone else. What I speak of is my personal experience which formed my own beliefs. There is an ancient Hebrew scripture in the number one NY Times best-selling book, **_The Holy Bible_**, which speaks directly to my heart concerning my mission and purpose in life. When I first saw this scripture, I knew that Hope dealing was my calling and purpose. I do not arrogantly share this personal revelation of my calling by any means; yet, I share this humbly and confidently.

Isaiah 61:

1 The Spirit of the Sovereign Lord God is upon me, because the Lord has anointed and qualified me to proclaim the Good News to the poor and afflicted. He has sent me to bind up and heal the brokenhearted and to proclaim freedom to the captives and the release from darkness and the opening of the eyes for the prisoners.

2 To proclaim the year of the Lord's favor and the day of vengeance of our God. To comfort all who mourn,

3 and to provide consolation and joy for those who grieve in Zion to bestow on them a crown of beauty instead of ashes, the oil of joy instead of morning and the garment of praise instead of a spirit of despair (a failing spirit). They shall be called Oaks of Righteousness a planting of the Lord for the display of His splendor.

4 They will rebuild the ancient ruins and restore the places long devastated. They will renew the ruined cities that have been devastated for generations.

5 Strangers (aliens) will shepherd your flocks, foreigners will work your fields and vineyards.

6 And you will be called priests of the Lord, you will be named ministers of our God. You will feed on the wealth of nations and in their riches you will boast.

SECTION 2

Hope for Those Whose Lives Have Been Touched by the Disease of Addiction

CHAPTER 1

The Sobering Discovery

I woke up late one morning to a bang, bang, bang! It took me a moment to realize that the sound was someone thundering down the stairs and running out the door. It was late in the morning, and everyone should have been either at work or at school. It was my oldest son, Nick! Why was he in such an urgent rush? Then later that day we'd hear from the other kids, "Where's my Nintendo?" "My PlayStation is missing." Then from my husband, "Where did my pressure washer go?" Hey, "Who took the paint sprayer?" We were clueless about how random items around the house began to disappear. Totally perplexed. Then one time . . . bang, bang, bang. I looked and saw my son tripping and falling down the stairs. Why didn't he have his balance, and why would he cry so easily? Why was he so moody and irritable? Why was he sleeping all the time at hours that people would not normally sleep?

One time, Nick's girlfriend at the time called me at work and asked us to check if Nick was in the house. I called home and asked my husband to look for him. He said he was not there. His girlfriend was persistent, "Look harder," she insisted. I called home again, and sure enough, my husband finally found him outside in his car, passed out in 96-degree heat. Pete pulled Nick out of the car and saved his life. But, why was my son passing out? What is going on? I've never experienced drugs before, so I was completely ignorant of any of *the signs*.

This is when we found out from my son, the words a mother never wants to hear, "Mom, I'm using heroin. I was really upset one day over an issue with my girlfriend, and this guy told me to just try this stuff to get some relief, and I'd feel all better. Well, I tried it, I felt better than ever, but now, I'm feeling really sick."

That was the beginning of an almost 7-year roller coaster journey that hit me upside the head out of nowhere, and inevitably changed the course of everyone's life that was involved. **My son was addicted to heroin.**

The opposite of addiction is connection.

My son was disconnected. One of the greatest challenges that I *never* expected, nor asked for, was to be the mother of a heroin addict. When my oldest son, Nick, went through his substance abuse journey, at first, I did not want to have anything to do with it. I had *zero* tolerance, I kicked him out of the house. I didn't understand it, I assumed addiction was a choice, and I had no clue it was a disease. I just drew a line in the sand, and I *shut him out.* I thought that I was doing the right thing by practicing "tough love" and that I was doing a good job of being a responsible mom by putting up a boundary because I had a younger son, Jordan, and a younger daughter, Julia, that did not need to be around any type of substance abuse in our home.

In some ways, I suppose I was doing the right thing; however, I really lacked a basic understanding of the disease of addiction. Little did I know at that time that I would go on a journey that lasted almost 7 years. Thankfully, there were seasons of peace and no drama throughout, but then there were those climactic episodes of active drama that could last up to 2 weeks. It was a cycle that seemed to occur about every 6 months.

It was one of the most challenging experiences to go through when binge-like episodes of the disease would erupt. It was terribly unbearable. I kept trying to block it out, and figured if I was strict enough, he'd stop using it. Why couldn't he just make a choice to *just say no*? It was clear I knew **absolutely nothing** about this disease. I didn't quite know how to handle this because my strictness was not forcing him to make better choices. I brought my kids up with excellent family values and Christian principles. I'd bring them to church, and a very supportive extended family surrounded us.

Nick always had this little rebellious flare to him as a child, but overall, as a child, he was sweet, fun-loving, extremely intelligent, and had a hysterical sense of humor. He still does! He struggled with some occasional behavior issues, from time to time. We found out much later that it all traced back to untreated ADHD and lower dopamine levels, which interfered with his ability to learn in school, causing him to have academic challenges. I remember in church, the children's pastor, Pendleton Brown, seemed to connect so well with Nick. Pastor Penn was the best children's pastor and musician ever! He formerly played Riff Raff in the Hollywood hit "Rocky Horror Picture Show" in his B.C. days. He truly understood it was hard for Nick to sit still and learn. He gave Nick a pogo stick and let him jump around in the back of the room while he sang his rock-n-roll scripture songs with the rest of the kids during children's church. Nick can still tell you all those scriptures to this day.

My other 2 kids, Jordan and Julia, had not one bit of tendency towards drugs, their behavior was stellar, so why him? The kids were brought up in a very blessed, positive, educated, and fortunate environment. I didn't understand. *I just don't get it.* Why is my oldest son going through this horrific addiction, but my other 2 kiddos were doing exceptionally well? I was totally confused.

CHAPTER 2

Jordy Goes to Jail

Let's reverse back one year before this shocking discovery, well before the heroin nightmare began. My husband and I were on the other side of town when we received a call that someone was trying to break into my home. Because we were at least an hour away, we called the police to go ahead of us to monitor the situation. When we arrived home, we realized that nothing had been stolen. However, they did call an investigative team as they found remnant shavings of Nick's marijuana in the bottom of the trash can of Jordan's bedroom. Long story short, both my boys got arrested on the spot and were escorted to jail. Boy, was I ticked off! Nick had been goofing off with pot and Jordy had to take the heat! Jordy had everything going well for him—excellent grades in school, great group of friends, about to graduate, and here he had to go to jail for less than one ounce of marijuana (scrap shavings) at the bottom of a trash can that wasn't even his! It was his room though, so that's why they decided to arrest both; of all the stupidest things, I was so mad.

Eighteen years earlier, Jordan Porter was born smiling with a persistent grin that extended from ear to ear. He never stopped smiling, which was why we told him his eyes look a bit Asian because he just kept smiling all the time. His eyes took on an Asian appearance. He ate perfectly, slept perfectly, never cried, and continues to this day to exemplify the definition of Hakuna Matata. Jordan played all his sports, never got in trouble at school, was friends to everyone, and was the all-around, All-American boy.

When I named him Jordan, I knew the meaning was "to go down under, to descend." Not that he would go down, but that he would figuratively reach down to help others that were fallen or at a low spot to get back up. That's exactly what I've always witnessed Jordy do. He continually reaches out to all and makes friends with every 2-legged and 4-legged creature he ever encountered. I remember once when a stray dog was coming around our home, Jordy took him in for a few days, fed him, and named him Ruffy.

Jordy is just a class act, good-natured all-around chill dude, likable to all and always lending a helping hand. You can imagine my frustration when I saw Jordy go to jail. I immediately bailed him out. I was so angry with Nick for putting Jordan in this position. I left Nick in jail so he could think about what he had done. With my whole heart, I love my amazing sweetheart firstborn son, Nick, just as much as my other 2 kids. So don't assume that I loved him less by leaving him in jail; I just wanted him to wake up and smell the coffee!

Both the boys went through the pretrial diversion program for the incident. This is a program for first-time offenders to complete a list of obligations in lieu of sentencing. Meanwhile, Jordan and my stepdaughter Christina both graduated from high school together. Life went on as Jordan continued to work faithfully on his pretrial diversion agreement with no errors. I remember one summer, we vacationed locally in Destin, Florida, instead of leaving the country. We wanted to be safe, just in case the rare occurrence of Jordan's "drug court color" got called for drug testing. This way we could quickly drive back home to get him tested. And sure enough, wouldn't you know, the darn color got called. I personally drove Jordan 5 hours back to Atlanta to piss in a cup and then turned right back around to drive 5 hours back to the beach. It was noted that every single one of Jordy's pee tests was clean each time they called his color. What a waste of the county's resources.

One time, Jordan and Christina, who were truly just like biological sister and brother, decided they'd go to Savannah for St. Patrick's Day. The typical St. Patty's day roadblock occurred on Interstate 16, and the officer checked both their IDs. Jordan had a warrant out for his arrest! We had come to discover that the very disorganized probation office mixed up paperwork between Nick and Jordan. Long story short, Jordan got nailed again, this time for not completing the probationary requirements, even though he did. Nick did not do what he was supposed to do though, and the paperwork was mixed up with both the boys' names!

I was so pissed off with the solicitor when we got to court that day. They were picking on one of the best-behaved kids around. There are so many other people they should be disciplining, surely not Jordan! I was so irate at this moment that the probation office couldn't get their clerical act together, and that Jordan had to go through such an injustice, that I had a rare mama bear moment and ended up exploding in the solicitor's face. Note to self. That doesn't help. ***Do not yell at the solicitor.*** Even if you are right and they are wrong. That actually gets your innocent kid a 180-day sentence in jail because I decided to piss in the solicitor's corn flakes.

I thought I was going to die after hearing that ludicrously unjust sentence. We were expecting to take Jordan right home from court, and all this nonsense would be over with. My heart sank as I saw one of the most well-behaved innocent kids being escorted off to put on an orange costume in this 3-ring shi*-show for 180 days. Poor Jordy's face was so horrified at what was happening. We didn't know what to think. Nobody gets this kind of sentence with no previous record and after completing pretrial diversion so well! We were shell shocked. We were numb. I was confused. Jordy was so confused. Nobody got that sentence for crumbs of less than one ounce of weed that wasn't even theirs. Why did ***real*** criminals get released with no consequence, off the hook, but the good and the innocent must pay because of a clerical error? ***Pure injustice.*** This was a horrific mistake. I should have never shown my feisty Italian side to the solicitor's face.

Each day I would talk to Jordan on the phone, I would also video conference him from home constantly. We went to every single one of his visitations. We spoiled him with lots of money on his books, so he had plenty of snacks for himself and for him to share with others. We sent him packages from Amazon multiple times each week, so he had plenty of great books to read. I had post-it notes numbered counting down each day until Jordan would come home. I frantically tried to work with the attorney to try to appeal or do something. It would cost us almost $10,000 to sue the probation office for their careless mistake. Jordan, in the meantime, unsurprisingly had such great behavior, he was immediately accepted into the workforce, and that credited his time as 4 for 1. Thank God, only 60 days later, the day before his birthday, Jordan was released! I immediately got tickets for him and his buddies to go straight to the Atlanta Braves game to enjoy his birthday.

For a long time, I'd think about how angry that injustice was. Sixty very long days for my fantastic son to have to serve for something he was **not** guilty of.

This is **exactly** why it's so important not to have anyone in your family who is struggling with anything illegal or active addiction (even though it was not heroin yet) in the home around their younger siblings because this kind of nonsense is bound to happen. It unfairly affects and disrupts the other kids' lives, to say the least.

I do remember Jordan telling me about a man who worked in the kitchen with him on the workforce. This older man was just about to be released when his mother had passed away the day before his release. How horrific to miss saying goodbye to your mother by one day! Jordan told me that he was able to be there for the guy and talk to him and offer support to a friend at a very difficult time for this man. I smiled and remembered why I had named him Jordan. This was why. I was proud of Jordan that God used him to reach down and offer kindness to another.

I have no doubts that Jordan probably made a positive impact on many other inmates during his short visit at the Cherokee County Detention Center. He always had a shining positive attitude, and he was very likely a light in the darkness. He made the best of a crappy situation, and I was so proud of him. I was no longer angry about the 60 days. Everything happens for a reason. There had to be some purpose.

As for Nick, whose name translates as "man of victory," he was *still* working out his journey of fulfilling that meaning. He ended up going back to jail for not doing his pretrial diversion. He stayed in jail about 30 plus days until I got him out by having him transferred straight to a rehab instead. Instead of jail, Nick ended up attending two of the best treatment programs ever, Hopequest first, and then to Timothy House for a total of 9 months. He looked great when he was finished. His mind was sharp, and his amazing personality filled with humor had returned. I was overjoyed to bring my entire family together again on vacation in the Riviera Maya just outside of Cancun. Nick was great. I felt so thankful to have him around and back to normal again. Not everyone's loved one makes it through treatment. This awareness made me feel exceptionally grateful. What a great kid, and what a gifted counselor he had become too! He'd help everyone talk through their family issues with such skill throughout the entire vacation. Little did I know, the addiction nightmare would soon return, multiple times. And with each comeback, it became fiercer and stronger.

Three Supernatural Encounters

G oing back a little in time, at about 1 year into the heroin addiction on my son's 19th birthday, he was standing at the kitchen counter with a young lady who was his girlfriend at the time. I looked up at them, and my vision went a bit blurry and blinding, all I could see was a whitish type of light behind this young lady. I wasn't quite sure what was going on exactly, but for some reason, I chose to surrender to the entire experience. All of a sudden, a vision flashed in my memory of a supernatural experience I had 20 years prior when I was pregnant with Nick.

I had been driving down 75 South by Lakewood Fwy when I had that same type of whitish blur occur. I felt a very warm smooth sensation pass from the top of my head through my entire body. I couldn't see well, and that warmth feeling became so intense that I was forced to pull over to the emergency lane. I was about 20 years old at the time. I stopped, and all of a sudden this fervent prayer came over me. All that I can remember coming into my head was a thought to pray like Hannah did (in the Bible) over her unborn child when she dedicated him to God. I figured, "Ok, I'm dedicating my son to God." I will roll with this. It was just an intense prayer that came out of my mouth out of nowhere dedicating my son to serve God. Startled, I thought, "Whoa . . . where did all this come from?" This silent voice that seemed to resonate in my thoughts said, "Do not worry, do not be afraid, I have plans for your son. He will go through a very difficult time. But trust me, I have a bigger plan, and he must go through this challenge in order for him to come out successfully on the other side. All of this is to fulfill my purpose and calling that I have on his life." After wondering if I had lost my mind for a split second, I had a peaceful moment as I silently responded, "Ok God, I trust you. Probably won't be too bad. We are up for the test. We can do this for you, God."

What I was really thinking was that maybe we'd go through some type of health challenge or illness or some type of tumor with some miraculous healing and that everyone would be inspired and say, "Wow! God healed this boy!" And God would use that to show everyone that He is the real deal. I collected myself back together, got back on the road, and never thought about that experience ever again, completely forgotten until 20 years later. The memory flashed before me as if it had just happened. That whole memory was restored to me like a picture-perfect movie reel replay. Not sure how long I was zoned out, it may have been only one minute, but all that flashed before my eyes in that one minute.

As I regained consciousness, I stepped back, shook my head, blinked my eyes, and remembered *at that moment* that any bit of worry, anxiety, or concern I had ever had completely disappeared. At that moment, I felt filled with a supernatural faith and hope that my son was going to be fine and that God is sovereign. He's in control of this situation. God still sits on the throne, and God's got this. This was His plan all along! My only job was to remain in faith and hope and belief in the promise God made to me 20 years prior.

I had an unexplainable certainty from that moment forward that I could in essence "sit back" and watch all the events unfold to God's glory. Ever since then, I've experienced this tremendously unusual peace that supersedes all understanding. Needless to say, the husband wasn't quite exactly on the same page, but how could I expect him to be? Pete hadn't had the same experience I had 20 years prior.

The series of events would continue to progressively worsen over the next 6 years, but I continued to hold on to this peace, faith, and hope that this was all part of the *plan*. My husband would always say, "You know, a very small percentage of people ever make it through a heroin addiction, and all the odds are stacked against him. My friends are telling me the outlook is not good here." I'd get so frustrated, I'd scream, **"Well, get you some new friends because these ones obviously don't know my God! I have a promise! You hear me? I have a promise!"** Honestly, my husband just did not understand how I could have peace and hope. Understandably so. He'd always say, "I gotta give it to ya, I don't know how you keep having this hope." As time passed, the episodes with my son would continue to get worse and worse, rehab after rehab, relapse after relapse. And Pete would say, "It's not getting any better, it never will, the odds are against him." And I just kept persisting, "You don't understand, it's going to be ok. I have hope, I have faith, I have trust that my God is still **bigger**! Remember, it's all part of the **plan** . . . we just need to walk through this and get to the other side knowing that God is with us through it all."

In the meantime, I had surrounded myself by people who had mastered mindsets. I remember Wayne Nugent, the CVO and founder of our company saying, "The only way through is through." And Jefferson Santos, one of my greatest mentors saying, "When you are going through hell, don't stop and pitch a tent! Keep going till you get out!" Not sure Pete ever quite grasped that though, and I'm not sure that I could've ever grasped that had it not been for those 2 supernatural experiences.

Then came experience number 3. I've learned over time that when anything occurs in 3's to pay attention, it's a sign. Nick along with my best friend Meredith, mentioned at the beginning of this book, went to downtown Atlanta to a celebrate recovery meeting. As they were walking down the street, a man, who called himself a prophetic artist, approached my son. This man asked Nick if he could draw a picture of him. And so, he did. My son brought this picture home. It was remarkably unusual. The last time my son came home with a colored picture was kindergarten. *How strange*, I thought. The interpretation of the drawing confirmed everything I had heard from the previous 2 experiences.

PROPHETIC DRAWING INTERPRETATION
- ever since Christmas you've been dealing
w/ danger, problems, issues, your path
is curved so you can't see what's
ahead, but by faith know that what
is ahead on the path is a red door
which means you are going to come
out in the end with great power,
the green grass signifies you will
bring life to others and this will be
worldwide impacting, you gift that
you can't see now will be
known worldwide.

My mind was blown! I now had 3 supernatural divine experiences that came together, that solidified and cemented my faith, hope, and trust once and for all that God's got this. He provided perfect peace to my heart and my mind in the midst of one of the ugliest raging storms imaginable. I could not be shaken.

CHAPTER 4

Experiences as a Mother of an Addict

Being the mother of a son in and out of active addiction and recovery has got to be one of the hardest struggles that I could have never imagined in a million years. The episodes were so difficult to go through. Even though everyone has a different experience, some readers may too closely identify with the following scenario. A cycle of heavy drug use would occur, followed by really weird erratic behavior that resembled nothing like the true personality of my son. Over time, I began to recognize these signs as an indicator that he was using. Extremely odd unexplainable erratic behavior, falling down stairs, extremely emotional, the crying, the theft, items missing all the time was endless. That was not the personality or character of my son whatsoever, and it just surprises you so much at first. Then, after it happens so many times, you begin to figure it out. The cycle would begin with total shock, and then we'd see the signs, then right away we'd discover that the addiction was active. After a while, the total shock part disappeared as I'd learn to quickly see the signs and know instantly what's happening.

This binge could go on for 2-3 weeks, until he would run out of money. Next came the inevitable withdrawals, then off to detox hopefully followed by rehab. We learned that immediately after an addict leaves detox, the first thing they want to do is use again. So, if they don't go directly to a rehab after detox, then they were just buying 5-

7 extra days of being off of heroin while enjoying other heavy meds that helped them detox. It seemed pointless if my son didn't get rehab or help immediately afterward.

At that time, he did not have any insurance; most addicts don't. We didn't know about Obamacare insurance at that time, so I had to always creatively find money for rehab *(they can be extremely costly)*. Most people cannot even afford to get treatment for their loved ones. It felt like survival of the richest. If a person didn't find a way to pay for treatment, they were out of luck. Today, however, more affordable or free treatment options are available than ever before. Thank God the government combined with communities have recognized this epidemic and have begun offering more assistance.

After a few times, we began to learn this cycle: the 2-3-week binge, then the 5-7 days in detox. Over and over and over again. The reality is that those 5-7 days feel so relieving to parents. It gives them a few days to breathe and not worry about their loved one overdosing. For a golden week, it gives parents a break from worrying if their worst fear will come true. That is the vision of the officer showing up at the house or the dreaded phone call with the news saying their loved one has been found somewhere overdosed. Then come the continual thoughts of exactly how this overdose possibility could play out. If not careful, it can consume and overtake the mind. Everyone who has a loved one struggling with addiction goes through those thoughts and scenarios constantly. Thank God I had that strange peace that I mentioned before. I could have easily gone insane otherwise.

Honestly though, that detox was such a relief knowing that for 5-7 days, we'd get a break from that underlying worry. Then, each time he was released from detox, the hovering concern started all over again. Sometimes he'd go for a few months and it would be great. Or he'd get on a round of Suboxone, and that would buy us 4-6 months of him getting his life back, working at a job, earning some money and restoring a little bit of what could be perceived as "normalcy."

We discovered later that the Suboxone was never a real long-term solution. Suboxone is buprenorphine, a prescribed medically assisted therapy given to those diagnosed with Opiate Use Disorder. It's still an opiate, so they still have the euphoric "high" that they are longing to feel but prevents the addict from overdosing. So, one opiate, Suboxone, is just safely replacing the more dangerous opiate, heroin, that can lead to overdose. It's a temporary crisis solution or a "band-aid" that gives the addict a chance to breathe a little, maybe tread their head above water for a moment. It's a chance to experience a little bit of normalcy in hopes that they will possibly come up with a plan to mentally, physically, and psychologically get their brain working right again. This way they can have a chance to get to meetings, therapy, or counseling to learn how to live a lifestyle of recovery. Medically assisted therapies are amazing because they keep the addict alive in crisis, but without counseling or other treatment plan options, it's just simply a temporary solution, and certainly does not cure the problem at all.

There was one particular scenario I witnessed more often than not. I noticed that when many addicts would get triggered, they'd just want to use again to cope with the triggers. Most addicts know that money can be made from selling their Suboxone. So, there we go again. What do you think a heroin addict is going to do as soon as cash is in their hand again? Buy dope. Use again. The cycle is continuous. Back to detox, back to rehab for 30 days if you're lucky, and each time you are hoping it's the last. Always hoping that something this time would be different. Pleading with God that the treatment *this time* would actually stick.

In a previous chapter, I had mentioned a time when my son was in jail. That was one of the best things that could've happened because he ended up being court ordered to go to rehab. If he didn't do his rehab program, then he'd have to go back to jail. This forced him to stay in rehab. He went to an amazing program at Hopequest which was one of the most solid and balanced rehabs I've ever observed. He then continued at another fantastic treatment facility for 6 more months at Timothy House. This facility was up in the mountains which got him away from the city.

After completing those programs, he was healthier and looked more fantastic than ever. His brain was functioning well again, so he decided he'd go to college and work on his degree in Behavior Addictions. I observed an amazing counseling gift that my son evidenced when interacting with others. He started out in his own apartment in Savannah, GA so that he could attend South University. When things would get stressful for him, I remember jumping in the car and making that 5-hour drive just to make sure he was ok on multiple occasions. The college experience became so stressful for him that it brought him right back to using again. I pulled him out of college and out of his apartment that was trashed beyond disgust. We spent hours trying to restore his apartment to normalcy so that he wouldn't be assessed fees from the apartment complex. He managed to rescue a little black puppy, Jade, along the way. Years later, I still primarily care for Jade as she has become part of the family.

We arrived home, and back to detox. We tried sending him to the remote mountains of Colorado to stay with his step-sister hoping he could not get his hands on any heroin. That was short lived. They had their differences and failed to get along. She ended up leaving him alone so that she could travel, and there he was, left alone unsupervised, off to find heroin again. I immediately tried to get him a flight to get straight back home where he could have some type of supervision. He was so deep into a binge again, but this time with no one around for hundreds of miles. I had to hunt down help somewhere, somehow. I came across a Lyft driver in Denver, named Donna. She was an angel to help search for him on the streets of Denver in hopes that she could get him to a safe place for me. Thank God she finally found him after searching all night! I tipped her generously—what a hero! After I had purchased 3 different flights because he kept missing them (with no refunds), he finally made it on a flight home with his emotional support dog, Jade.

Here we were, back on the hamster wheel. He'd be ok for a little while, then stress occurs, and right back into using again. Every coping skill he had learned in rehabs and with counselors seemed to be flushed right down the toilet.

CHAPTER 5

Tough Love and
the Traveling State Fair

The addiction finally arrived at a point where I became so done, so cooked, and so roasted you could stick a fork in me. Overall, I still clung to my peace and hope, but I was getting exhausted. I wanted to keep him safe. I wanted to be there for him. I wanted him to feel loved and accepted. I didn't want him to go through this alone. I was the mom that was always there for my kiddos. But enough was enough yesterday!

So, we made an agreement. I offered to help him out with a car if he would try out this rehab, Bethel House, deep in the mountains of North Carolina, far away from any civilization or drugs. If he wanted help with a car, then he would have to try this rehab for at least 2 weeks. Maybe, just maybe, I prayed, it would stick this time.

After only 2 days, he was calling me to pick him up. He didn't like it. I said no. I was sticking to the 2 weeks no matter what. Anyone could try something for two weeks, right? The problem was that he just wasn't ready yet for rehab and recovery. He ended up bolting from the rehab and ran until he found his way into the little mountain town. There he came upon a homeless shelter. He called me and told me to pick him up at the shelter. It was hard, but I stood my ground and absolutely refused to enable him. It's not 2 weeks. He gave me hell about being a horrible mother, abandoning him and leaving him up there in the mountains.

He'd call me several times and share a few choice words laced with guilt that any decent mother would not abandon their son like I was doing.

There his bottom stayed at the homeless shelter. Period.

I had already decided in advance that the only involvement I would have, without compromising my own boundaries, would be to talk to him on the phone. This was so that I could continue to speak loving words and life over him. I would also offer food to him. So, he'd have to find a phone to call me, wherever he was, and he did. I also regularly had pizzas delivered to the homeless shelter. I never felt bad about giving him food only. I had a feeling he was the only resident at the shelter who had a mom regularly having pizzas delivered. But I would not give him money, nor would I drive up there to pick him up. That was HARD. I was proud of myself that I stood my ground.

I knew that figuring it out on his own was what needed to occur. No more mommy bailing him out and fixing everything for him.

One day, he called informing me that the traveling state fair came through town and offered for him to fill out a work application. Shortly after that, he was working for the state fair. He traveled with the fair through North Carolina, Tennessee, and then wouldn't you know, right back home to Georgia. I knew the address of every fairground that he'd stop and work at for a few days because I'd have to give the address to the pizza delivery guy every time.

That boy ended up amazing me. I did *nothing* to get him back home, and he figured out a way to get himself right back home to Georgia. He will tell you to this day how proud he was of himself for finally figuring something out on his own.

One day, while working at the Cobb County fairgrounds, he called me and cried, "I'm back mom, but now I'm sick." I immediately drove up to the hospital and met him there while he was treated for pancreatitis. He wasn't using heroin at this time; however, he replaced his addiction with alcohol and was obviously drinking too much with his coworkers. He ended up getting fired from the fair for drinking. There he was sitting on the side of the road outside of the Cobb County fairgrounds in the pouring rain with his bag of clothes. He called me to pick him up. It killed me, but . . . I said, "No. You got yourself into this situation, you still must figure a way out.

Papa, his grandfather, who is my dad, surely couldn't stand the thought of his grandson being out there in the cold rain, so he picked him up and helped him out for a night because I would not allow him to stay at our house. After that, Nick's best buddy Tanner told him to go and try living at Sober Living America in Atlanta so that they could be there together. Those 2 boys were like frick and frack, in and out of SLA in Atlanta, then Tampa, then Atlanta again.

The number of vehicles and car accidents that my son went through at this time was mind-boggling. We have this great benefit of emergency roadside service with our travel club . . . we have multiple accounts and ended up depleting **all** of our freebies for that year. Tows, car in the ditch, flat tires, no gas, keys locked out . . . it never ended with my dear son. I also remember the Legal Shield membership we **overused** that always provided an attorney at no charge for most of his situations. They always went to court for my son and got him out of each mess. Between Legal Shield and Emergency Roadside Service, I was definitely receiving the full value and monies' worth. I likely saved thousands of dollars. Even Nick's doctor, Dr. Richardson, had later come to say, "Boy, you have dodged more bullets and have had more free passes than I've ever seen."

By this point, when it comes to financially managing a child with an addiction, I had it all figured out like coupon mom on steroids. I had discovered every short cut and resource to save money with legal, emergency roadside, insurance, scripts, hospitals—you name it, I was forced to become super resourceful. These unsolicited skills came in handy later on when offering multiple support services to addicts through my nonprofit. See? There you go. Everything happens for a reason.

CHAPTER 6

Wake Up Call

There was a period during the journey when my son was living at Sober Living America halfway house in Atlanta as his addiction lifestyle became too disruptive to the others at home. Nick was on a recovery streak after another recent heroin binge when we received the news that Nick's best friend, Tanner, overdosed and died.

I could not believe or accept this news at first. Tanner was a long-time friend to our entire family. He was like a son to me. He had great friendships with all of my kids in the family, including our family dog, Daisy. Tanner even created a Facebook page for Daisy that exists to this day. I remember so many times I would frustratingly stick those two jokers, Nick and Tanner, in my car at the late-night hours and drive them to Highland Rivers detox in Cedartown. They would spend 5 days there detoxing, receiving treatment to alleviate them from getting "dopesick." Again, it was normal for most addicts to go straight to "dopemans" house after detox if they weren't sent straight to rehab. I still had a hard time grasping this whole addiction thing.

Tanner's overdose devastated all of us. What a sweet heart Tanner had . . . why? Why him? He was one of our favorites. He'd go through seasons of sobriety and be so proud of himself. He'd come into my house smiling and saying how well his recovery was going. Now he was gone. There was nothing we could do to bring him back. I hated this with a passion. I really ferociously hated heroin. Heroin is **pure** direct evil in a liquid form that entered people through a needle.

There was a huge spike in overdoses going on at this time in our community and all the surrounding suburbs of Atlanta. Heroin had risen to epidemic proportions, but none quite hit home as strongly and as intensely as the death of Tanner. I remember jumping into my car and driving down to Atlanta to the Sober Living Recovery House. I needed to be the one to share the horrific news to my son that Tanner was gone. We all together froze in shock, disbelief, and emptiness. ***Pure devastation***. That was the initial wake up call for my son. Nick finally began to actually consider treatment for himself. It wasn't the end though. The active addiction kept cycling for almost 2 years to follow that it took 2 or 3 more episodes of relapse before a noticeable change occurred.

CHAPTER 7

The Understanding
of the Disease and MAT's

After Tanner's death, my whole perspective of addiction changed. I began a quest to educate myself and commit myself to deeply understanding addiction. I learned that substance abuse begins as a choice, but then there biologically comes a point where substance abuse is no longer a choice. It switches over into a disease called addiction.

I learned that this condition is actually in the DSM, labeled as substance abuse disorder. The DSM is the medical book published by the American Psychiatric Association that is used to diagnose and cover all categories of mental health disorders. I began to learn about mild, moderate, and severe opiate use disorder. I gained a greater understanding of the disease of addiction. The addict often comes to a point where they want to stop, they don't want to use anymore, but they still use. At this point, it has become a disease. No matter how badly they want to stop using, they can't stop without their body requiring the drug or else they will become painfully sick, aka "dopesick."

They *need* the opiate to keep from going through a horrific process in their body called withdrawals. It has been found necessary by medical professionals that these withdrawals be medically assisted and supervised. I really began to develop compassion towards those who struggled with this disease. Before this awareness, I had always judged drug addicts for not having enough will power to make a choice to stop.

Again, it is a choice in the beginning to use, but it quickly evolves at a certain point into an illness where it's no longer a choice. It is truly a physical, mental, emotional, medical, psychological, and anatomical addiction in every way. Again, no matter how badly they want to stop, and most do want to stop, it's almost impossible to stop on their own without help and a lot work to enter a lifestyle of recovery. It requires tapping into and connecting with the higher power that the addict chooses to identify with in order to survive the disease of addiction.

There is hope. There is life after addiction. There is a way through. The addict can get to the other side. It is necessary to consciously participate in a recovery lifestyle for the rest of their lives. Honestly, I think it's a great lifestyle for anyone to choose to live. There is freedom from addiction.

Every time we'd go through another episode of horrific binge use with my son, I'd remind myself of the Source that comes from above that gave me my strength. The peace, the hope, and the trust never left my heart. Thank God. I don't know how families get through addiction without God. I guess sadly, some just don't ever get through it.

Tanner's death also awoken Nick to the realization that he was going to die if he didn't do something. It felt as if all his friends around him were dying from overdose. Funerals became a regular Saturday activity.

Shortly after that, we had learned about a Naltrexone implant through a YouTube video that my amazingly resourceful sister, Noelle, had shared with me. Apparently, you could get this surgical implant, and it would block all heroin from being absorbed, resulting in no way to get high which led to no way to overdose. Wow, could it be true, I wondered? A magic cure?

$17,000 was the price tag for a 12-month ticket of worry-free life. No overdosing. No heroin use. One problem, **no** insurance that would cover it. I didn't even know any addicts that could afford health insurance anyways at this point before Obamacare came out. I was resourceful though. I persisted and determined until I found a way. I never took no for an answer. My son's life was worth way more than the $17,000 that I didn't have, so I'd have to figure out a way. I was determined that if there is a will, there is a way. I will not subscribe to the unjust "survival of the richest" plan.

My parents generously helped out with the down payment, and I financed the rest. Done. God provided. Nick proceeded to experience 12 months of a steady job while living successfully at SLA. By the time it began to wear off, we had discovered that the monthly Naltrexone shot, Vivitrol, which used to be $1,500 a month, had recently been covered by insurance! Wow! Before that, Vivitrol was for the wealthy. Heck, insurance was for the wealthy (or the employed—not many addicts kept a job). It had previously been part of the "survival of the richest plan." That pissed me off. If an addict wanted a chance at living, they'd have to be rich.

Out of all fairness, there is the daily naltrexone pill, which was fairly inexpensive, but let's be real. Does anyone know an addict that remembers to take a pill every single day? If you miss one day, then it does the addict no good. Naltrexone was not like Suboxone. It was non-addictive and had no euphoric side effects. Therefore, if an addict got triggered, they would just skip taking that pill that day and use again. The pill was a waste of time for most. However, the monthly naltrexone shot was awesome. You couldn't forget to take it because it was monthly, and it was non-addictive!

I remember Tanner telling us once about how he wished he could afford the Vivitrol naltrexone shot. It made me so mad and so sad and so infuriated that insurance didn't help out with Vivitrol until after Tanner passed. I imagined he would have done so well on it. I was very angry about that for a long time. I became passionately fueled about lack of finances keeping people from getting the help that they need. Here we are in the richest country in the world, and addicts are dying left and right. What an injustice. What a healthcare crisis! Sadly, society was still at that point of unawareness that addiction is a medical issue and a diagnosed disease and should be treated as such.

Thank God when Obamacare came out. Thank God. I didn't give a rat's behind if one voted for Obama or liked Obama or any political opinion for that matter. Obamacare was truly an answer to prayer in the lives of so many. Every addict at that point could finally afford good insurance to get a doctor and get a script for these life-saving MAT's (medically assisted therapies). As previously shared, MAT's are not the ultimate answer, but again, they offer the band aid to stop the bleeding in crisis so that the addict can get level headed enough to work on themselves permanently.

Next obstacle—average people could not understand how to navigate the very grueling confusing marketplace application on healthcare.gov, much less a struggling addict whose mind was still foggy. I became more and more consumed with thoughts about all the ways we could've helped or saved Tanner. I kept getting more and more mad that I couldn't help him more. This was a driving force that caused me to devote my time and energy to find ways to support addicts practically in their struggle and recovery. I was determined to find a way. There is still hope. I became determined to help others navigate that confusing website!

CHAPTER 8

The Therapeutic Recovery Project

Between the Naltrexone implant and the Vivitrol shot, we were set for a season of at least a year and a half. Nick had a great job. He left SLA and came back to live with us in the mountains as he had a good bit of sobriety under his belt at this point.

I had now begun to gain more understanding and compassion towards the disease of addiction, while simultaneously keeping in the forefront of my mind that everything happens for a reason, and everything has its purpose. I was open and receptive to God placing on my heart the undertaking of a massive project that would later come to be known as: The Hope is the New Dope Guatemala Bottle School Project.

I called my friend, Kit Cummings, who I've mentioned previously, and shared what God had impressed upon my heart. Kit was in complete agreement to join forces and trust God to take this project full throttle forward. This project's objectives would serve a dual purpose.

1) We would co-create a therapeutic recovery service project for recovering addicts in hopes that adventure travel combined with serving (voluntourism) would facilitate these addicts to experience true dopamine production resulting from serving others.

2) We would co-create a memorial for Tanner and others loved ones lost to the disease of addiction.

We had been part of an innovative travel club that offered trips that combined travel with volunteer service projects (Voluntourism). Our club partnered with an organization in Guatemala called Hug It Forward that leads groups of volunteers into remote cities in Guatemala to build eco-friendly schools. These schools are constructed with walls insulated with plastic water and soda bottles that are filled with trash. We chose to use the club's platform as a vehicle to take anyone whose lives had been touched by the disease of addiction on this innovative experience.

While we were on this trip, we had a memorial service for Tanner and dedicated the school to him. We took handwritten notes and pictures of Tanner and placed them on the dirt floor before we poured the concrete over them to form slabs. This way a piece of Tanner would always remain in this school forever. We also dedicated this school to all those that anyone in the group had loved or lost to the disease of addiction. We also had the opportunity where recovering addicts were strategically positioned to experience the joy of serving others, causing the natural dopamine rush mentioned previously that would occur when creating a smile on someone else's face.

A perfect opportunity was created to experience
a natural God-given high without a substance!

In addition, we were familiar and comfortable with the safety measures and excellence that our club implements when putting these programs together, so it was *all systems go*!

A group of 20 of us journeyed to Guatemala. Addicts who were once called *"worthless piece of crap junkies"* in the USA, were now called *"heroes"* in a remote village in Guatemala. The community had no judgment nor knowledge of these young adults' past struggles. All they knew was that someone was coming to serve them and make their lives better by building a much-needed school for their community along with playing, laughing, and smiling with their children.

> ***Imagine the tremendous impact on the self-esteem***
> ***and self-worth of the recovering addict.***

I considered doing a local service project, which would also be amazing. However, with heroin addiction being such an intense and severe disease, I figured that extreme actions of ripping the addict out of the USA and placing them in a completely radically different environment would produce an extreme effect. I wanted to attempt to match the activity with the extremity of heroin addiction. Ultimately, I was shooting for an extreme recovery activity to counteract the extremity of the drug somehow.

Almost a year was spent fundraising the $40,000 it required to make this project materialize for 20 people. That was a massive undertaking and amount of money for us to raise. We all felt greatly challenged as we attempted to sell candles and solicit private donations. I stepped aside from my own efforts and finally had a conversation with God. *"Look here God, you placed this vision in my heart, I need you to work out all the financial details for this project."* Shortly after that conversation, a larger corporate donation arrived, and the trip was now really happening!

Pete, Kit, the whole gang, and me anxiously packed our bags and zipped off to Guatemala to witness the Hope is the New Dope Bottle Guatemala Bottle School Project come to full fruition. We actually co-created a therapeutic recovery activity and combined it with a heartfelt memorial while witnessing God perform this marvelous orchestration.

CHAPTER 9

Our Buddy from the Ditch

About a week before our trip, I noticed a post on Facebook from a mother who had lost her son to heroin overdose 2 years prior. She was requesting prayers for her other son, Kenny, who was in detox for heroin. Kenny was found 5 days earlier face down in a ditch overdosed and was in treatment. It was time for him to be released from detox the very next day. The mother was expressing concern as to what to do because he could not return to her home as she was raising Kenny's young son. Kenny's mother had a responsibility to keep her grandchild in a drug-free environment. This had to be a difficult decision to make between her grown 26-year-old son and her 7-year-old grandson combined with the grief of the recent loss. The mother had no choice but to do what is in the best interests of the grandchild's well-being.

This is an all too common challenging situation that most families of addicts deal with constantly. For a mother to be in a position of having to choose between their struggling loved one and the well-being of their family at home is a decision that no mother should ever have to experience.

After reading this post, I immediately glanced over to my son and said, "Hey Nick, isn't Kenny one of your friends?" Nick responded, "Yeah yeah, he's one of my friends, yeah, we've used together before. You remember mom, he came over to the other house a couple of times before, you gave him that Prayers Answered Immediately Book?" And then I remembered.

In the back of my mind, I'm still thinking, *ok . . . so this must be Nick's chance to be used by God now and help someone else. Here's his purpose . . . the purpose is now about to make itself known. Great, we are right in sync with the whole master plan. Nick is actually at a good point during this time in recovery.*

I beamed at Nick and said, "Hey, Pete is out of town, it's just you and me here for the weekend, so what do you think about us going on a mission and driving down to Cobb County at the detox? We can pick up Kenny since no one else is really in a position to bring him home right now."

Since we lived up in the mountains at that point, I thought bringing him back home with us will help him get away from the city for a bit, hopefully far enough from *"dopeman."*

"Nick, we could try to help him, encourage him, and maybe he'd even want to go to Guatemala with us. I know it's a longshot because it's only a week away, but maybe he can get on the trip with us! We can try. Anything is possible with God. You never know what God wants to do."

Nick exclaimed, "Sure! Let's go get him. I'm all in with that."

So, the very next morning we jumped into the car and drove to the detox. We entered the facility and stated we were here to pick up Kenny. We sat in the waiting room while they called him up. Sure enough, Kenny came out gasped, "Whoa Nick Porter . . . what's up man?" Nick immediately responded, "We're here to get you, man." Kenny kind of laughed saying, "Yeah, right."

He proceeded to go outside to look for his mom's car, as he assumed she would pick him up. Nick pleaded, "Really man, we came to get you." I interjected, "Kenny, really, remember me? Nick's mom? I spoke with your mom, and yes, we **really are** here to get you for real." Nick confidently proceeded, "I'm clean now man. We wanted to come get you to see if you wanted to stay with us a few days at our house in the mountains while you figured things out." Kenny said, "What? Nick Porter clean? No way man . . . I thought you were there in the waiting room because you were waiting to go into detox!"

I shared with him that his mom couldn't take him back into the house right now because his son was there and it wouldn't be allowed, so we are here to try and help out. Then Nick said, "Here's the way I see it man . . . I know you want to go to *"dopeman"* right now. I know you want it right now. I know. So you got a choice. We can bring you to *"dopeman,"* drop you off, and you get what you want. Then you are on your own, it's up to you from there to figure out where to go. Or, you can take a risk, give us a chance and come to our house in the mountains for a few days to think things through . . . How bout it?"

The guys stood outside the car for a minute while they smoked a cigarette in silence. No pressure. No pushing. The choice had to come from Kenny alone. Kenny got back in the car and responded hesitantly, "I *do* feel like going to *"dopeman's,"* but I'm going to take a chance. I wanna try to do the right thing for my kid . . . all right . . . I'll try it . . . you sure y'all ok with it if I come up there for a few days?"

Nick and I smiled. About halfway back to the mountains, I told Kenny that he could only stay for a few days because we were leaving for Guatemala in 6 more days, so no one would be home to stay with him. I cocked my head, lowered my voice and nonchalantly said, "Unless of course, you want to go to Guatemala with us."

We then explained the two-fold initiative with the Hope is the New Dope Bottle School Project, clearly defining the objectives of the therapeutic recovery activity and the memorial for Tanner. He surprisingly looked at us saying, "Are you serious? Dang that would be cool if I could go, but I can't get a plane ticket, don't have a driver's license, no passport, no money, nothing, and I have a court date. There's no way that can work out." Well, that was the trigger that pushed my *challenge* button because obviously Kenny did not know my God the way I know my God, and the God I know can make anything happen. Challenge on!

I briefly grew quiet as my brain flashed back to a memory 2 years prior, when my friend from Iceland, Heidny, sent her son, Stefan (little Tiger Woods) with Pete and me to a company event in Denver, Colorado, several years ago. We were at the end of our trip and were rushing back to the airport to catch our flight. **Problem! Oh No!** *Stefan forgot his passport on the pool table of one of the R.A.T. Packers, David Townsends house where he had been hanging out. If we turned around and went back, we would surely miss our flight.* **Oh no no no!** *We were not missing our flight . . . heck no . . . no way . . . no how. I thought . . . God's got this. He knows I cannot miss this flight. We are going in and we are all getting on that flight no questions asked. Period.*

I confidently told Pete and Stefan no problem . . . me and God . . . we had this discussion and we've got a plan. Please understand, I really wasn't being arrogant. I was just being confident. I needed a way to get through Stefan through TSA security without ID, and only God could pull that off. I briskly instructed, "Pete, you go ahead through security, and Stefan, you follow me quickly; do exactly what I say." (I really had no clue what to do yet . . . I was just going with the flow waiting for inspiration of a plan to be revealed). The way security is or at least was at the Denver airport is that the TSA agent was right there where you initially put your bag through. So Pete showed his ID, went through, then I showed my ID with Stefan behind me. I then slightly cracked open my suitcase and pushed it a little extra hard on the table, so it fell on the other side of the TSA agent. As all the contents spilled out, I said, "Oh no . . . Stefan, help me pick all this up!" It was a masterful diversion divinely inspired, and there was Stefan doing exactly what I said. He quickly went through to help me pick up my bag, passing the TSA agent, as the agent's head was turned to see the contents of the mess. My husband's eyes were huge, and I gave him a look that said, "Look straight forward and keep walking buddy." Stefan and I gathered my bag, picked it up, and just kept walking over to the Xray scanners without a word! Phew! We made it! Now if God can get Stefan past a TSA agent with no identification, then He can surely orchestrate all the events that needed to happen to get Kenny to Guatemala with no problem. After all, He is the God of the Universe. (Disclaimer: this is not ever acceptable to attempt bypassing security, but the intentions were spontaneously innocent at that moment. No harm, no foul. I have no intentions of ever attempting nor encouraging this again.)

Memory flash over, back to the story in the car with Nick and Kenny. After having that memory flash, I exclaimed, "Kenny, God willing, **you are going to Guatemala**, just watch God move the heavens and the earth just for you dude because He will. I've seen him do it before. Just roll with it."

We arrived home, blew up the air mattress, and Kenny grabbed a spot to sleep in the downstairs apartment. The very next day was his court date. He got through it successfully. His mother then met us shortly after that with his birth certificate. After that, he went to Dept. of Driver Services and obtained a new license which was required to apply for a passport. Lastly, we drove to downtown Atlanta to the passport office on Peachtree Street. By the time we arrived, we were late.

The office had already been closed for an hour as we were long past the appointment time given to us the night prior on the automated system over the phone. The security guard looked down at my purse and recognized a hand sanitizer on there that was branded with the name of our travel club, and blurted, "Oh, you're part of that . . . me too! Just go on in; someone should still be in there that will take his application." So, he let us through to the passport office! We ended up walking in to be happily greeted with absolutely no wait because they weren't taking any more appointments at that time. But one woman behind a window graciously announced, "Come on over here, let me see if I can't help you." We turned in all his papers and application without any questions and showed that he had a last-minute flight confirmation that we had just booked. Routinely she said, "Come back tomorrow and his passport will be ready for pick up."

We left and returned the next day, Kenny ran in, picked up the passport that was ready, and ran right out! *Hot dog! That was unreal! All those events came together seamlessly!* So many obstacles: the flight, the drivers license, the passport, the addition of him onto the trip at the last minute with the trip coordinator and getting through the court date all miraculously in a matter of 2-3 days. Kenny was on that plane first thing on Sunday morning on the way to Guatemala with the rest of us! *Done! Phew! Go God!*

CHAPTER 10

The Sweet Community of San Martin Enhanced with "Lil Skye"

The Guatemala experience was indescribable. The friendships created were magical—lifelong friendships that exist to this day. The community was so grateful to have us there. We worked on our assigned section of the school building project with the other adults and children in the community. We all played with the children and came to know how sweet and precious each one is. The community flowed together so beautifully in spite of the dirt floors and the absence of all electronics. The tortillas were all handmade from corn flour. Eggs were freshly laid from chickens. Everyone seemed so unified and appeared so genuinely loving towards one another and to us. What a refreshing experience to come into such an indigenous beautiful culture in San Martin. They woke up when the sun came out and went to bed on hard dirt floors with blankets when the sun went down. They were surprisingly content even without a mattress to sleep on! There was no modern furniture, yet they were happy! I'd hold sweet young children in my lap as I watched Chris, Nick, and Kenny race the kids in the wheelbarrows. I peacefully observed as Lulu braided all the little girls' hair and swung in the hammocks with the children. I watched Jayden, Julia, Jesse, and Amani sing and dance with the children and pat together tortillas with the older ladies and children in the little houses.

In addition to the wheelbarrow rides and races given, we enjoyed playing soccer with the kids which was their main activity. The community had its own soccer ball. Just up the pathway from the school site was a small field made of dirt, where they regularly played soccer. All the kids assembled in unity and played together.

I recall this adorable little girl in the group who was noticeably different from the other little girls. All the other young girls had their traditional Guatemalan skirts with the belts wrapped around. This little girl was not dressed that way. She wore cut off shorts and had short hair. She didn't have that long braided hair like the other girls did. She also wore a denim type vest over a white t-shirt. Her appearance was different, clearly unlike any of the other girls. Sitting beside me on the bench on the field was one of my best friends, Skye. Skye is one of the most amazing individuals I've ever known. She is the coolest lesbian right up there with cousin Helen who was also on the trip with us. I looked over at Skye and playfully exclaimed, "Look, they've got their own little Skye in the community here too. She's just a mini version of you!" Skye laughed.

Now here's the cool part: I observed the culture to be very conservative, and so I asked one of the guys who was helping lead this trip, "How does the community treat this young girl? How do they receive her here in such a traditionally conservative community? Did she ever get teased or ridiculed like she would if she was in the USA?" The trip leader's response was very confident, "Oh no, they are family here, they are all one community; they accept everyone as they are and for who they are. They are all part of the community, and this is not an issue. It would not even occur to them to even make this an issue. Here everyone is family. That is who she is, and that is how she expresses herself." He then reiterated that she is part of the community and they all treat each other like family and allow each other to be who they are with no judgment. Skye and I were both so touched by the purity and love in what we had just heard. We were fully aware that in the USA, this situation may not always work out quite like that. Our hearts were warmed—what a beautiful picture of love that still remains in mine and Skye's hearts today.

CHAPTER 11

Post Guatemala Hopedealing Efforts: Caves, Planes, and Segways

After returning to the USA, we all experienced a bit of culture shock as we were plunged back into reality. Many of the participants expressed their desire to stay longer; some even wished they could live there. They could not wait to return again one day. However, in the meantime, we had to figure out how to function in reality where American Society was faster paced and more stressful. Society in the USA was more tainted with judgments and stigmas towards the disease of addiction. Life was about to get real, and challenges were inevitable.

Oh, how we all longed to have that loving, unified culture, absent of prejudice, as mentioned with the little girl in the prior chapter. I felt it would be effective to start support group meetings each week, along with adventure activities every so often, to hold us over until we could return to Guatemala. This is where the early conception of our 501c3 nonprofit organization, Hopedealers Worldwide, really began to form. It began with initially taking the group to Guatemala in November of 2016. After returning, we began meeting together. First for New Year's Eve, then on Sunday nights with a themed support group and relationship building objectives.

We also planned extreme dopamine producing activities to keep the action going. One time, we all participated in an extreme caving adventure. Many of us were so surprised when we saw our buddy, Chris Nikolaisen, arrive in Atlanta from Houston, TX, to join us on the Tennessee caving excursion. What a fun surprise. The gang hadn't seen Chris since our Guatemala trip. It was a fantastic weekend connecting with one another again. It all centered on our slogan, "The opposite of connection is addiction." If our organization could create a connection between one another in the community, then hopefully it could help people maintain the recovery lifestyle. One by one, new friends and faces would become part of our little culture. A very inspirational recovered addict, James Hatfield, discovered us on Facebook and became part of our family. To this day, James, once known to be one of the hardest core addicts, reminds us of how important it is to be connected with others in the community who are actively pursuing a lifestyle of recovery. A precious young couple, Casey and Abby, found us through a friend, and became part of our fam! Amani brought her friend, Sagar, and many others came together on a weekly basis after the Guatemala trip. We called ourselves ***Hopedealers***.

It is very common for the recovery experience to sometimes include relapse. I remember one time right around my son's birthday, Nick and Kenny were so very tempted to relapse. I remember somewhat teasing them, "So you guys wanna get high? You really wanna get high? Ok, no problem. I'm going to take you to go get so freaking high, you will never forget this. So they got in the car with me, and we drove up to Chattanooga Skydiving Company. I convinced them to put their restless butts in a little bitty plane that flew up to 14,000 feet in the air. I recall my son reciting the serenity prayer as the guide shoved their butts out of the plane at 14,000 feet skydiving. That there was their high, their adrenaline rush, their dopamine creator, that no drug would provide for them. This ended up being another little adventure on my quest to give these guys ways to experience a natural drug-free high.

Another adventure experience we all enjoyed, was going to downtown Atlanta on a Segway tour. We zipped all through Atlanta and enjoyed learning about the cool stories the tour guide would share with us from the old Oakland Cemetery in Grant Park to the restored and reformed community of Inman Park, through the campus of Georgia State University, and to my favorite: the Martin Luther King National Historical Park. Here we spent time absorbing the inspirational history center, the birthplace home, the reflecting pool, and the eternal flame. Again, whatever fun and wholesome activities we could do to create the synergy of the natural dopamine experience, we would do.

The Documentary, The Cinnamon Culinary Masterpiece, and Our Beloved Friend Shelly

There was one dear friend of ours that attended our Guatemala trip that went in proxy for her sister, Shelly, who was severely struggling with heroin addiction. Shelly had also been a dear friend of our family for years, since the age of 15 or 16. She was one of Nick and Tanner's best friends. I remember going to a Christmas party that she had put together with homemade cookies and special decorations. She had one of the sweetest and biggest hearts I've ever known. Sadly, her weight appeared to be down to about 85 lbs. Her eyes were sunken, and she appeared extremely weak. My husband exclaimed, "My God, it looks as if that precious girl is knocking on the door of death. I can't imagine her surviving another 2 weeks."

This really alarmed me when my husband said this because we had just lost Tanner, the year prior, and I could not imagine another one of the family friends losing her life to this horrific disease again! Her body seemed to be dwindling, her teeth had been decayed, and we had never seen her so thin and frail. She was in crisis, and I was not about to sit aside and watch us lose another sweet loving soul. I tried my hardest to see if she could get into a rehab.

As with most families, the money is not easily accessible to pay for these $25,000 a month rehabs. These treatment facilities seemed so ridiculously overpriced. Families and friends of loved ones have depleted their life savings, remortgaged their homes, and scraped every last penny just trying to pay for rehabs because as mentioned previously, most drug addicts don't have health insurance. Even so, health insurance doesn't always cover the much needed medical and psychiatric treatment and rehab facilities that these struggling addicts really need. Sadly, rehab and recovery facilities are truly out of reach for most addicts.

I fondly recall a very precious memory of Shelly. One day, I was visiting her house and I had not yet eaten dinner. Her frail, tired body walked down the stairs and insisted on preparing me chicken and sautéed vegetables. She meant to put salt and basil on the chicken. Accidentally, she ended up sprinkling cinnamon and basil on the chicken. She had a look of horror on her face as she apologized, "I'm so sorry Nadine, I'm so so sorry! I accidentally put cinnamon on the chicken, oh no! I meant to put salt, oh no it's ruined!" I assured her not to worry, maybe it would taste good, and sure enough, her "little culinary accident" ended up being the best tasting cinnamon and basil chicken I had ever had! Oh my God, it was so delicious! Her "accidental dish" ended up being a culinary success! That was so awesome. She was the best!

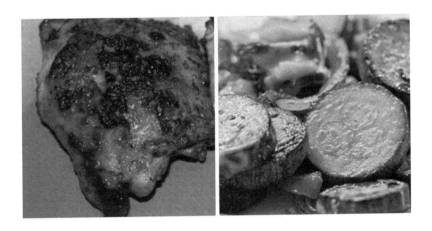

Right around this time, I had heard that a popular national TV show was considering doing a documentary on some of the stories of addicts in Atlanta. I reminded myself that only 1 in 10,000 applicants was chosen to be on this show, but if I could just get her on that show and they could follow her case study, then I know it will end up with her being sent to a top rehab that could help her. **The rehab would be paid for!** That was the whole point of getting her on this show. The entire goal was to make one last extreme effort to get Shelly out of the bowels of Atlanta and into a really nice rehab on the other side of the country to help her receive the treatment that she so desperately needed for no cost to her or her family! It would be far enough away that with a little hope and faith, she could get her life back together again!

I began banging on the phone lines of the producers of the TV show pleading with them how desperate Shelly's situation was. After several repeat phone calls and emails, I finally heard from one of the producers who considered taking Shelly's case and allowing her to be on the show! My persistence and determination for doing this were not to promote myself on national TV by any means. I did this to get her to a rehab in hopes of her getting her out of crisis and restoring her life as soon as possible. They agreed to meet with her.

I was so thankful that finally I felt a ray of hope that she could live again. We all painfully got through that documentary, and she got to that rehab for free. She gained her weight back, and she looked healthy again. We were so proud of her. She had a wonderful several months after that and looked healthier than ever. Sadly, the following winter, Shelly suffered from an asthma attack and passed away at the young age of 25. God must've decided her soul was so sweet that He brought his precious angel, Shelly, home to heaven to be with Him.

Another great loss to us left the earth that day. Our hearts were once again shattered—First Tanner, then Shelly. I'm reminded of a scripture in Isaiah 57:1 that says, "Good people pass away; the good often die before their time. But no one seems to care or wonder why. No one seems to understand that God is protecting them from the harder time to come." Tanner and Shelly both were two of the sweetest, most kind hearted thoughtful young adults I have ever met, and their loss was deeply painful to us all. Their memory lives on forever as we continue to celebrate the good memories we've had with them.

CHAPTER 13

Relapse after Relapse, Spiritual Entities, Love Always Wins

After the filming of the national TV show documentary, my son decided to skip his Vivitrol shot. He got in a fight with his girlfriend. He expressed he was sick and tired of not feeling "normal." He shared that life was too hard for him to live sober. Heroin would make him feel normal again. It gave him the dopamine he wanted to feel just to feel normal again he'd say over and over again. Here we go again.

Nick went through another relapse. Police were called because the disruption that occurred in the home would often get volatile and unsafe. By this point in time, I was very aware that these behaviors were not characteristic of my son. It seemed as if a demonic entity had overtaken him. The DSM would label it: ***substance induced psychosis***. When this happens, I know better than to interact with my son. He would be completely detached from who he really is. To argue with him would be like arguing with a dark spiritual entity . . . clearly not my son. To argue with my son whose brain is altered by substances is pointless. 1) he wouldn't ever remember it and 2) it's really not him at all. It became futile to engage. I began to clearly see the entire episode as a completely spiritual interaction.

Immediately in my head, I would silently hear that scripture in Ephesians that says, "For we are not fighting against flesh and blood, but against evil rulers and authorities of the unseen world, against mighty powers in this dark world, and against evil spirits in the heavenly places." In a previous chapter, I shared that when I was a child, I had experienced the spiritual realm that was more real to me than reality itself. Yup, that was it . . . right here. That's what I'm talking about. I would often see the spiritual realm more real than reality. I think that was my saving grace. Wisdom would tell me to simply stay quiet, yet firm and under control. Remain in love because love is the greatest weapon and always wins. And no matter what . . . **do not ever acknowledge or even react to the aggression coming from the dark side** through my son. I gave it no energy. I would not ever stoop down to that level of even giving it attention.

Unfortunately, my husband didn't quite see it from that same perspective, so it was more challenging for Pete to manage his reactions. However, I knew what I had to do. I had to clearly and quickly, with ultra-controlled laser focus, look straight forward amid crisis episodes. My head could never waver from side to side. I'd grow this unshakeable backbone and stand 10 feet tall. I would give calm, clear, and authoritative directions, and I always kept boundaries for safety first. Never once would I give the "dark side" the satisfaction of me reacting adversely or losing my cool. Not once. There would be NO satisfaction of a "reactive" response from me whatsoever. Police were often called at this point to protect physical altercation from occurring between my son and my husband. Safety first. My "son" would get so upset and blow up and drive downtown to get more dope, threatening to overdose. I used to yell silently in my head, *"Who are you and what have you done with my son?"* But then, I'd remember to use my spiritual vision, and all would make sense to me. All I could do at that point is to pray with confidence and authority.

My son would call me sometimes, and I could barely understand his slurred voice from being so high and nodding off. One time, my dear friend in our travel club community, Officer Paul Hodges, was on duty in Atlanta. I was thankful to be able to call Paul to ask him to find my son when my son was parked in his totally wrecked truck and nodding off in a very dangerous area. Thanks to the "find my friends" app, I could give him a fairly close address. I'll never forget how kind Paul was to sit there with my son until I could arrive from the mountains. I am so grateful for friendships.

After that, I remember my son being on such a heavy binge, he would go down to The Bluffs (the biggest most dangerous drug dealing area in Atlanta). Many who went into the Bluffs never came out. My son was so desperate to get more dope at this point, that a gang member who was a dealer offered my son free dope in exchange for being a "tester" for different kinds of dope with fentanyl in order to test the strength of this particular concoction. This is how sick and deeply twisted this disease can get! The worse binge ever! At this point, I was beside myself, just praying, not knowing what to do. It felt as if it was the ***dark side's*** last strike out against my son to try to get him one final time with the worst situation ever.

I lay on my bed praying, wondering how much longer before we come out on the other side of this journey? Could it get any worse? Conflict in the family. Conflict in the marriage. Jordan and Julia were both fed up with the episodes of their older brother. I only wish they could've seen it in the perspective I saw it. That would've helped for sure. It gets lonely so many times to feel like other people can't see things the way I see them in the unseen realm. When I meet others who can see in this "spiritual realm," I get so excited because finally, someone understands what I see! It seems that most don't see this, so they don't understand, and it's ok. I've learned to accept that I'm just different in this way. I'm not better than anyone by any means. Just different.

It was hard for anyone to really understand this disease anyways much less expect anyone to digest the whole ugly package that comes along with it. I remember praying and telling God that I still fully trust him, and he's got to handle this because, at this moment, I've run out of options. I was exhausted. I knew that if I kept running down there to Atlanta rescuing him, I was just enabling him, and I wasn't getting anywhere. I was done making trips down to Atlanta. ***Done***. At that moment, the phone rang.

A previous contact, from the recovery industry, was calling to let me know about a private investigator/adult sitter company just in case I ever knew anyone who needed that service. This service is contracted by families who cannot find their loved one that is in active addiction and potentially in a dangerous situation. Their guys hunt down and professionally care for the addict until they are delivered into a safe, stable situation. It helps families who are trying to keep a healthy personal boundary but still need some intervention to help keep their loved one safe. I collapsed in the chair thinking, "What perfect timing!" I need them right now to find my son.

I ended up hiring this company who, on the spot, sent out 2 guys that were pros. Displaying a perfect undercover appearance, two recovered addicts tattooed from head to toe, looking like they fit right into any sketchy situation began the hunt for my son through the bowels of Atlanta. They stayed on search duty 24/7 until my son was found. They brought him back to his house and kept 24/7 watch on him along with every move he made. They hid his phone and truck keys and purposefully did not tell me where they were hidden so that there could be no chance of my son talking me into getting them. They stripped him of every privilege and freedom except food, shelter, and clothing.

I'd never witnessed such an extreme operation. This was militant die hard. It's what was needed. My son could go nowhere and had no options except to rehab. The negotiations went on for 24 hours. I didn't have to do a thing. These guys were pros and handled everything masterfully, all the way to Blue Ridge Mountain Recovery, where my son was taken to rehab. The guys did not leave until they were certain he was settled. Now I was blown away. Talk about removing all the stress from me and getting exactly what I had wanted to be handled perfectly by professionals. It protected me by keeping me out of the direct scene.

Wow, I thought, *this amazing service is probably going to cost me close to $500 or something close to that. But it will have been worth every penny.*

The contract came in over the email. My husband, until the day he reads this book, does not know I was shocked with a $3,500 bill for this service. Well, there goes that credit card blown up to the max. Love you Peetie. Thanks for always loving me in spite of . . .

Again, I had to surrender to the fact that my son was in a dire situation in the armpit of Atlanta and he is worth more than $3,500. If you total up the entire expense of everything that entails living with someone that struggles with the disease of addiction, I can bet you that after rehabs, services, meds, lost work, stolen items, lost time, etc., we were looking close to an average of $50,000 **with** insurance. Some families have remortgaged homes, drained entire savings, lost marriages, pawned cars, sold everything they had to deal with a loved one's addiction. This is no joke. This disease is truly horrific and extremely costly in every way.

After that, my son's addiction was managed for a short time again with suboxone. Then stress hit him once more. Suboxone sold, cash in hand, then relapsed again. We found him upstairs in the bathroom, fallen off the toilet, pants down, *(way more than I needed to see there)*, needle still in the arm, back in the addiction. This time the relapse was over in less than 24 hours. We had since moved only a few streets away from my parents, so I called them over. It was time for *some "grammi marital law."* Their solidity and foundational strength of over 50 years of marriage now, was the experience we needed to draw from. They are aware of spiritual principles and we all armed ourselves with the biggest prayer covered, wisdom-filled, love bombs ever imaginable.

Somehow, someway this time, the "pixie dust" of Grammi and Papa was just what Nick needed to reach his heart and knock some sense into his head. It worked!

He chose to go back to his doc and has been on different meds and has worked on his recovery ever since. It's been a long time since that last relapse happened. To this day, he is still under the regular supervision of his doc and still benefits from MAT's. He maintains a great job and lives in a nice home with his very beautiful fiancé, Tiffany. She has never used heroin and will never tolerate my son ever using that as a coping mechanism, should he ever fancy that idea again. She has a good heart. Those two can get crazy sometimes, but overall, they've got it together, and my son is doing well, clean, and sober to this day.

One aspect that remains consistent with my son through this whole journey is that he has *always* taken responsibility for his actions. He has ***consistently*** come back around after each episode to sincerely apologize for all the disruption he has ever caused because of the addiction. He has always been so remorseful and humble. I know who my son is. I've always seen him through God's eyes amidst all of this. However, I've recognized a noticeable change in his heart and in his actions where he really has decided now to grow up, better himself, and move into a level of maturity and responsibility that was not apparent before. He's even in classes now to become a Certified Alcohol and Drug Counselor. Thank God!

Of course, I'm deeply thankful to God. I sometimes feel as if I never give my parents enough credit for all the fervent and intentional prayers behind the scenes that *I know* they are responsible for. My parents are my silent warriors. They never need to let the left hand know what the right hand is doing. They are heroes of the faith. I'm so thankful to God for my parents. My children also know how blessed they are to have pillars of strength, wisdom, and love that can always be counted on and has always been found through their whole life in their grandparents, Nick and Dianne Blase. The best parents and grandparents ever, hands down, unanimously agreed upon without question by all the kids and grandkids involved. Heroes. Not perfect, but they know the One who is perfect. They've got the connection also, and it's not just because they are Italian either.

CHAPTER 14

The Breakfast Club Classes

Shortly after Shelly's passing, the TV show episodes with her story and our organization aired. It was bittersweet. The bitter part was that Shelly had just recently passed the week before the national airing. The sweet part was how many lives had been touched and impacted by her story. Many struggling addicts reached out to our organization asking for help. We were able to be there for many by providing them the resources that helped guide them in getting the treatment they so desperately needed.

After the show had aired, someone approached me and asked, "What are you doing working around and having a nonprofit organization dealing with a bunch of struggling addicts without any type of certification or credentials in the substance abuse field?" At first, I thought, "Do you have to be certified to extend love to someone?" But then, I started feeling like I got caught with my pants down and I very quickly took to heart the valid point that was made. I remained intentional to have certified and experienced counselors and speakers conduct our support group meetings most of the times such as Greg Griffin, Kit Cummings, and other people with experience who know what they were doing. It wasn't always feasible though to get someone to come in and lead our meetings, so I stopped the meetings for a season and put the entire mission of the nonprofit on hold until I felt a peace about what we're to do next.

Yes, we still could fundraise for the next Guatemala trip, but in the meantime, I was determined to get my Certified Alcohol and Drug Counselor Certification. I began the journey of working on my CADC to bring further credibility to my efforts with those who struggled with addiction and recovery. What evolved from there was a transformation of the objectives of Hopedealers Worldwide. As I began to attend required workshops that commenced at the crack of dawn on early Saturday mornings, I started to feel like I was in the Breakfast Club with the variety of people I grew to know and love over the next couple of years. Unlike the Breakfast Club, our certified instructor that we hired was an old friend of mine, Tony Reynolds, and he fits right in with our crowd and connects and laughs just as much as we all do, if not more. People in our class are from all walks of life. However, I was surprised that several of the students were recovered addicts. These people who became my friends soon thereafter, were champions of the disease.

They were not only bettering themselves with education and certification to acquire a job that provides an honest living, but they are moms, sisters, dads, and real people who have come out victoriously on the other side of the struggle. They had decided to pay it forward and make a career of sharing with addicts how to get "out of the hole." Many had previously burned all their financial bridges and were spending their last few dollars that they really couldn't spare, just to have a chance at swinging the bat in life and taking the shot to make something of themselves. A lot of their money or family's money had been previously burnt up with rehabs, not leaving much room for extra monies to pay for an education in hopes of getting a solid, higher paying job. In addition to that, they had the experience to back up their education which could only be a recipe for creating the best counselors ever. This inspired our organization to offer educational scholarships to those who met certain guidelines and kept specified commitments. This allowed the financial burden of the cost of the CADC classes to be somewhat relieved. This is an amazing career that I became aware that many recovered addicts had in their hearts to pay it forward and help other addicts get a breakthrough. I've included the following poem that seems to describe it best:

AN ADDICT FELL IN A HOLE...

POSTED BY SAMIAM IN DIARY   ≈ 3 COMMENTS

AN ADDICT FELL IN A HOLE and couldn't get out.

A businessman went by and the addict called out for help. The businessman threw him some money and told him to buy himself a ladder. But the addict could not buy a ladder in this hole he was in.

A doctor walked by. The addict said, "Help! I can't get out!" The doctor gave him some drugs and said, "Take this. It will relieve the pain." The addict said thanks, but when the pills ran out, he was still in the hole.

A well-known psychiatrist rode by and heard the addict's cries for help. He stopped and asked, " How did you get there? Were you born there? Did your parents put you there? Tell me about yourself, it will alleviate your sense of loneliness." So the addict talked with him for an hour, then the psychiatrist had to leave, but he said he'd be back next week.

The addict thanked him, but he was still in the hole. A priest came by. The addict called for help. The priest gave him a Bible and said, "I'll say a prayer for you." He got down on his knees and prayed for the addict, then he left. The addict was very grateful, he read the Bible, but he was still stuck in the hole.

A recovering addict happened to be passing by. The addict cried out, "Hey, help me. I'm stuck in this hole!" Right away the recovering addict jumped down in the hole with him. The addict said, "What are you doing? Now we're both stuck here!!" But the recovering addict said, "Calm down. It's okay. I've been here before. I know how to get out."

It was cool how all this came together, and at the time of writing this book, our organization has been able to scholarship more than 28 students so far, just in this past year.

A good friend of mine who is a licensed insurance broker, Bill, guided me on how to assist many active struggling addicts, recovered addicts, and their families with the confusing process of navigating the Obamacare Marketplace health insurance. It was a game changer to see how many people were able to finally get affordable healthcare on their own. Those struggling could finally have the means to get a medical doctor, medically assisted therapies, and rehabs! Relapse is very real and is very common during the recovery process. I know my son relapsed 8-10 times before he maintained sobriety for a significant amount of time. With the insurance, the docs, scripts, and rehabs now mostly paid for, all that financial stress was one less thing that had to be worried about.

CHAPTER 15

The Philosophy, The Mantra, and Our Buddy John

Over time, I realized that I have this "superpower" which is accessible and available to anybody who has the courage and commitment to tap into it. As one of my business partners, Troy Brown, once stated, "It's not for the few that are chosen, but it is for the few that choose." It's simply a conscious choice if I want to exercise my ability to use this "superpower" or not.

When I share this "superpower" with you, please understand that my intention is not to come across arrogantly, yet just to only come across confidently. Arrogance would say that I'm better than others. Confidence would say that nobody is better than me. This "superpower" is for the few that have the courage, character, commitment, and the heart of love to want to carry out the mission of love. What is this "superpower?"

It is the ability to see another person through God's eyes. To look at others for who they really are beyond all their circumstances, mess, flaws, imperfections, offenses, and wrongs. I have painfully committed to cultivating over the years the ability to see people the way God views them. Not easy. But fulfilling and liberating. I realize I am not a "chosen one." I am simply just one who chose to be an open and receptive vessel for God to use me. One attribute about this gift *(because I am human, and there is always the ego, that humanity inevitably struggles with)*, is the ego which is the very factor that would keep me from seeing someone the way God views them. It's the ego that can keep me from speaking to someone the way that God (or Love—since God is Love) would speak to them. When I have interactions with people, ego can keep me from interacting with them in the way that God Himself would interact with them. I simply view myself as nothing more than just a human extension of God's love through my eyes, my mouth, my hands, and my interactions. Because I'm in a practical human body and skin, I'm able to be a deliverer of the message of Love and Hope. A distributor for God's messages. A Hopedealer.

Often, I personally struggle with the selective use of this "superpower." For example, sometimes when the people I'm closest to or live with *(it could be my spouse, one of my kids, a person that I'm around a lot that I'm very used to)*, I very often do not exercise my ability to use this superpower because my ego keeps getting in the dang way. That darn ego *(stands for **E**dging **G**od **O**ut)* keeps me from exercising this superpower with my husband, children, or others I'm close to. So many times I find myself being used by God to exercise this ability with people that I **don't** see regularly, or people that I'm **not** necessarily that close to because then my human daily living issues with my ego don't get in the way . . . so it's easier. However, I'm at a point in my journey where each day I've committed to do my best to remind myself to have an ego check so that I can use my "superpower" with those that I'm close to, especially my spouse, kids, family, or friends that I'm close to.

A large aspect of the ego that hinders me from exercising my ability to see, speak and interact with others the way that God would are these two: judgment and pain body entities. Judgment is the opposite of love and compassion. As much as I try to say to myself, that I'm not a judgmental person, these "pain bodies" can sometimes creep in. Pain Bodies is a term used by Eckhart Tolle, a famous international author and speaker. They are defined as a previous unhealed hurt within your heart from a previous experience that every human deals with. When I unconsciously form a judgment, for example, against my spouse, it's more apt to happen because of a previous past hurt or experience I've had in my past. If I dig deeper, I can work with a coach, counselor or sometimes just on my own, in my personal reflective time to identify this pain body. I can strategically focus on tracing this bad *(well, I don't want to use the word bad because the words "good and bad" carry judgment in itself)*, so let's say non-life producing fruit, and trace it to a root where it's originating from. If I can trace it to the root in my own reflective time, through the help of what I would refer to as The Holy Spirit, then awesome, if not, I get a coach or counselor to guide me. I can pull up the stinky fruit and then receive an awareness so that the judgment can go away. Then, the ego no longer controls or has power or blockage over the situation allowing me freedom to tap into my "superpower" again!

I see a constant cycle in my own life and in the life of many others that is a vicious cycle we can get trapped in. We first make an assumption, which is triggered or heavily influenced by a previous pain body. Then, that assumption immediately leads to a judgment which in turn immediately provokes an emotion or feeling, which is usually negative. This negative emotion or feeling feeds directly into an egoic reaction in lieu of a Godly or Loving reaction.

I don't want to lose anyone in terminology here, so let me clarify this upfront. I don't want terminology to stop anyone from hearing what I'm trying to express. I personally have a relationship with God through Jesus Christ who died on a cross for me and has displayed His love for me when I was not deserving of it. The power experienced through that relationship and awareness has been necessary to bring me to a healed condition in my heart. That awareness has brought my esteem, security, self-confidence, and identity to be founded in that promise of assurance and in that gift that God has offered to us. Some people may be reading this and thinking that *"Oh, she's a Christian and is trying to promote her religious philosophies and views."* Well, yes and no. Yes, I do profess to be a Christian. No, I do not project my views on any reader here whatsoever. This is my own belief and philosophy and I take that personally for myself. If someone is to come to that same belief, then they must come to that **on their own**, it cannot be convinced or projected upon them.

Exercising love and respect towards others, **no matter what another's beliefs are**, is my responsibility. Likewise, it is also my job to never judge or form an opinion towards others. I would be judging! My job is just to love, and out of that comes respect. I respect where anyone is on their journey at any point in their journey regardless of their philosophy. If I really dissected this, I could say that my philosophy and belief system is that of Love.

In my own heart, that love equates to God. God is Love and Love is God. The gift that God has given me through Jesus Christ and the promise of eternal life with Him is the ultimate display of love to me. The grace and hope that has been extended to me through what Jesus Christ did for me are what I perceive and define to be the greatest act of Love ever committed. If someone has a different philosophy, circumstance, or message, that's just simply none of my business to critique. That would bring me out of Love and into judgmentalism which brings us right back to ego, which would again, likely be heavily influenced by a previous hurt that was triggered by a past negative experience. My only job as someone who has devoted their life in service to God and God's mission of Love is to simply love. That entails having compassion, no judgment, and accepting people where they are on their journey.

The most logical example of anyone I've ever seen on earth display this more than anyone else is Jesus Christ. This is a big reason I identify with Christianity because I really appreciate the example that Jesus came and taught and exemplified for us. When those of other religious philosophies *(like the Pharisees and Sadducees)* were ridiculing and ignoring the prostitutes, "sinners," and anyone who was perceived to be a lowlier person, Jesus ended up having compassion on those who were perceived as the "lowly" ones in society. He extended love to them.

God created everybody; God created all things. Each person is created in the image of God. One of my wise friends, whom I consider to be a dear brother, Kit Cummings, said it in this way,

"Maybe our focus should be in finding the God within others, instead of focusing on bringing God to them."

So logically, if every person is created in the image of God, then their situation, circumstance, mess, wrongs, faults, and imperfections would all become irrelevant. Then it becomes my mission to look beyond all the dross and look for the God within others.

One day, I went to visit a young man in jail. John was a good friend of our family that yes, made a mistake, and was serving time for his offense. However, John still has a piece of God within him, and even though that may not be the predominant shining attribute at this present moment, the God within him *still* exists. I chose to remain open and receptive to be used by God, and it was placed upon my heart to go and encourage John. I would commit myself to find the God within him and look at John in the eye and speak the truth of what God truly is within him. Then I just roll with whatever else God wanted me to do or say during that visit.

We have this ability, with the ego set aside, inspired by what I define as the Holy Spirit, to look in someone's eyes and see them as God sees them, regardless of their circumstance, present appearance, or their present state. If God created John in His image, then there is a piece of God within John, and I was determined to allow God to use me to find it, verbalize it, and bring it out into the light. I went to affirm that hope and to remind John of the truth of who God created him to be and the plans, purposes, and potential God has for him.

I'm thinking, if all of us would just try this practice just once, we all could collectively change a lot of lives. Not just to leave an impression on others, but to leave an impact on others. Keep in mind, the impact isn't coming from us because if it came from us, it would just be ego. I am reminded that the impact is truly God inspired. The only thing we do is make the choice to set our egos aside and then be simply available to be used by God, drawing from the piece of God within us.

The visitation at jail went well. John was encouraged and began to have hope again. Shortly after that, my business partner, Tony and I went back to the jail and were able to administer a professional evaluation. After the assessment, Tony's recommendation for John was to leave jail and receive treatment in a rehab. I attended the bond hearing, handed the formal recommendation to the judge, and John was released from jail and has been thriving at the Timothy House for months now. Hope came through! The battle isn't over yet, but no matter the outcome of his future court date, John's faith and hope have grown strong enough to know that God is always by his side, and there is always *hope*.

The picture you see below sits strategically in my bathroom to the right of my toilet because logically, we all never skip the routine of using the bathroom each morning. Therefore, I cannot avoid seeing this picture each day. It is my daily mantra that I say regularly. I pray after reciting this mantra that each day God will help me to put my ego aside so I can be used in this way. And to do this, I have to pray for a lot of love and compassion towards others. I have to set aside hate, personal offenses, judgments, assumptions, and all those other yucky things that are inspired by the ego.

I have to identify all those icky thoughts and make a conscious choice to set aside those very real and valid human feelings. I must determine to make a conscious choice to choose the path of love, compassion, and hope which I pull from my higher power, which to me is God. So there it is. My superpower revealed. Seeing others through the eyes of Love in spite of . . .

It is a superpower available to anyone who has the simple awareness and courage to use it. Simply put, I'm just a friendly local neighborhood Hopedealer.

MISSION:

TO BE AN EFFECTIVE SERVANT LEADER, IT IS ESSENTIAL FOR US TO **REMAIN** IN THE LOVE OF GOD. WE HAVE TO LEARN HOW TO **SEE** PEOPLE THE WAY GOD SEES THEM. THEN, WE NEED TO LEARN HOW TO **SPEAK** TO THEM THE WAY GOD WOULD SPEAK TO THEM. OUR **INTERACTION** WITH PEOPLE SHOULD CAUSE THEM TO UNDERSTAND AND APPRECIATE WHO GOD IS AND WHO HE WANTS TO BE FOR THEM.

CHAPTER 16

Wrap Up

All of these events and many more all came together to happen for a greater purpose. Combined with my faith, hope, and the belief in God's sovereignty over all these events, I realized that without my son's addiction journey, there would be no Hopedealers Worldwide.

If my son had never gone through this incredible horrific struggle, I could promise you there would be no nonprofit organization that has helped so many people up to this point. Some might have not ever received help if we hadn't been there to support them. There might still be addicts out there with active addiction with no community to belong to, no insurance to cover their medical expenses, or no Vivitrol to keep them from overdosing.

There would be no Guatemala memories or experiences forever planted in the hearts of many. Perhaps without our initiative, there could have been many more deaths, hurts, struggles, and tragedies. Hopedealers Worldwide's initiatives truly have been a co-creation and collaborative effort by everyone involved.

So that leaves the unanswered question, "Why do bad things happen in this world anyway? Why does God allow certain things to happen the way they do? Why does God allow young people to die of terrible diseases?" All I can say in response to this question is to either read the book or watch the movie "The Shack" by William Paul Young. This movie gives an enlightening and indisputable explanation as to why bad things happen. It reveals an answer to this mystery greater than anything I've ever heard in my life. Just watch the movie.

We don't understand, we cannot comprehend, we cannot fathom why bad things happen, but all things do happen for a bigger reason, a higher purpose that we may never understand while we are on this earth. All things do come together in the end. I know I serve a God who has, still does, and always will sit on the throne. I've chosen to put all my hope, faith, and trust in that belief system which has served me well. God knows exactly what is going on and He is going to use all these things together for his purposes and glory in the end. I can now see that more clearly after viewing the movie above which will totally open your eyes to that concept.

I can tell you this much, when life decided to give me a bitter lemon of a situation, I was somehow determined to find a way to create lemonade. And without my son Nick, Hopedealers Worldwide would likely have never happened.

Hope for Freedom, Fun, and Fulfillment: Relationships, Business, Emotions and Spiritual Growth—The Community of Believers

CHAPTER 1

Spiritual Growth and Foundation

While attending the University of Georgia, working on my degree, I had a personal spiritual encounter in which I devoted my life in service to God. I remember kneeling and praying, "Here am I Lord, use me, send me." That was just before I went to work as a Camp Counselor during my first summer in college. Never did I realize that by expressing that one prayer, God would take me seriously. Honestly, had I known the lifelong sentence that prayer entailed, I may have reconsidered and bailed out from such a zealous request. I was so connected with this new found experience I had with God, I was sold out and would have done almost anything. Lots of zeal without much foundational knowledge is ignorance on fire.

I began my spiritual walk with God when I was a young adult. One thing I definitely learned is that I had much potential for growth and maturity. As a teenager, I began to dabble with spirituality during retreats in the Catholic Church. However, that felt more like a religion to me. The spirituality experience really took effect when I began to view my beliefs as a relationship with God as opposed to a ritual. I decided I wasn't going to be Catholic anymore because I didn't want to identify with a religious denomination, doctrine, or rules. I just wanted to freely be a plain and simple spiritual Christian, or what some may consider *non-denominational*. This practice of spirituality has continued throughout my life. I learned the value of practicing a relationship with God vs. practicing a religion. This served me well. Religion actually became the enemy as I began to learn and understand that religion, dogmas, and doctrines were more like the Pharisees in the Bible. These Pharisees cared more about their rules and their laws. Christianity was more about loving God and loving one another.

As a child, I remember during religious instruction in the Catholic church, learning about the 10 commandments and how important it was to keep all those rules. In this new movement of Love, where Jesus spoke of the 2 Greatest Commandments, (love God and love one another), I resonated with greater peace. I felt more connected to God and to others in a relationally focused way. My whole spiritual philosophy in life has resolved to understanding that the 10 commandments were not abolished, they were just fulfilled through the two new Great Commandments. If I could just focus on loving God with all my heart, and then loving one another, then all the rest is covered under that, right? I took that simple philosophy to heart.

Living amid the Bible Belt, I felt uncomfortable in the presence of around 95% of the churches located in Georgia. My heart always felt saddened because I didn't see people practice loving God with all their heart, and I certainly didn't see people loving one another. Was I too simplistic? I constantly questioned myself. I don't think so. My mind was made up that Love is simple. Humans have overcomplicated God and Love. God is Love. I actually started having a disgust and aversion towards religious organizations when I saw more hurt coming from them than Love. Although there is no perfect church, I did find some, few and far between, that were intentional about simply loving God and one another. These are the communities I noticed where grace was abundant, and judgmentalism was diminished. I thrived in those places where condemnation, rules, and judgment ceased to exist. I learned so much.

I am forever indebted and grateful to Liberty Church in Marietta, GA. I experienced tremendous growth through the teachings of John Fichtner, who is still the pastor there today. He delivered the *heart* of God with the most radically, passionate, truthful, balanced, and loving messages. I'll never forget some of the early teachings such as his marriage course. His worldwide distributed marriage course is what initially drew me to Liberty church. It was not your typical traditional religious marriage teaching. It was cutting edge, biblically sound, loving, Christian psychology. I learned that God is the God of all sciences including psychology. Any psychology I needed to know could be found in the Bible. Science is not the enemy of Christianity but science is created by God Himself. The cool part is that the more I looked into science, the more I'd find God. Wow. I considered the concept of Intelligent Design. Clearly, the most innovative scientific creation is the human body miraculously designed by God Himself. I learned that God cares more about human hearts than about religious rules.

To this day, I'm just so appreciative and grateful to the foundational teachings of marriage that John would reveal in a way that seemed so understandable and relative in today's society without compromising biblical truth.

All his messages seemed to boil down to the simple truth of loving God and loving one another. Then there was the DISC Personality Profile course that changed my entire perspective on how to deal relationally with ourselves and other people. In the company I work with now, we use something similar to understand personalities, called the "Colors" (red, green, blue, and yellow). Many organizations use other popular personality assessments such as the Myers Briggs Indicators. My first exposure to this entire concept of personalities was through the DISC course taught by Pastor John Fichtner. He shared that the four main different personality types were relative to the four faces of man in the Bible. It was so enlightening and fulfilling to me to finally understand who I was, and then to understand the personalities of others. This made so much sense. This was the psychology and wisdom that is the underlying basis of how to "love one another." It was so much easier to love one another if I could understand how to relate to myself and one another! I learned how to develop compassion, patience, grace, and love for those whose personalities were different from mine. All of the psychological personality teachings greatly influenced the person I am molded into and who I continue to become today.

I'll never forget the Racial Reconciliation series of messages. At this point, my mind was so blown away by the innovative marriage and personality teachings; I was eager to learn more. This revolutionary series brought a level of enlightenment and hope into a world that was still somewhat blind to this subject, especially in the South where racial tensions still existed. If anyone still had one ounce of racism in them after this series, then they must have been sleeping. I had been taught to be colorblind ever since I was small. I didn't grow up in the south, I grew up in New York, and for the most part, the culture up north was colorblind. In 1985, a trace of racial tensions was still noticeable when I moved into the Southern Culture.

I'm humbled each time I go to the National Historical Park of Martin Luther King Jr. MLK is one of my heroes right up there below Jesus Christ. Pastor John reminded me of a modern day MLK. John Fichtner delivered these amazing enlightening messages to us, his messages carried with so much power. It is the Spirit of God that I'd hear flow through this man because he opted in to be an open vessel and regularly surrendered himself to Godly disciplines that would clear out the EGO allowing God to flow freely in truth and power. I remember a time in that series where he explained things about racism that blew my mind. For example, John genetically proved that the first man on earth had to be the darkest skin pigment color because that's what followed the scientific laws of genetics. That was the first time I had ever heard that Adam, the first man on earth, had to be the blackest black man possible according to the science of genetics.

In a Southern state, smack dab in the middle of the Bible belt, that probably was not the most popular thought pattern going on in churches at the time. John was and still is very innovative and cutting edge. It was obvious how carefully biblical, scientific, and research-driven his messages were. His research was proven; there was no disputing such well-founded and sound truth. John is definitely one of the most gifted teachers ever, all he strived to make known was the genuine *heart* God has for **all** people. I remember at one point when John asked everyone who considered themselves a "white person," literally to take a moment and apologize for the sins of their ancestors to those who were "black people." It was a powerful and humbly moving experience. I'd strongly encourage everyone to listen to this series at libertychurch.org to get the full experience of the weight that this series carried. We learned that one could say that they have no racism in them whatsoever, but after you are done hearing this series, it may be revealed that a person discovers some racism inside that they never realized existed. The spirt of racism is laid out and unveiled so plainly and clearly. I deeply embrace the beauty that this revelation carried.

There was a season when the church collectively practiced scripture memorization. It wasn't a religious rule or anything like that, it was really a personal experiment in our own lives to observe and experience how scripture memorization could affect us. The wisdom behind this is to plant scripture in our hearts so that at any given moment in life, when needed, words of wisdom would just pop out as a way to conduct ourselves or successfully cope in any given life situation. I found this exercise, and still do, to be very effective. The first time I participated in this activity, the scripture was Isaiah 61, mentioned in a previous section. It was no mistake that this happened to be the scripture memory verse during the time that I was at Liberty Church. This scripture ended up being one of the puzzle pieces that fit into my life's purpose and calling.

> THE SPIRIT OF THE SOVEREIGN LORD IS ON ME, BECAUSE THE LORD HAS ANOINTED ME TO PROCLAIM GOOD NEWS TO THE POOR. HE HAS SENT ME TO BIND UP THE BROKENHEARTED, TO PROCLAIM FREEDOM FOR THE CAPTIVES AND RELEASE FROM DARKNESS FOR THE PRISONERS, TO PROCLAIM THE YEAR OF THE LORD'S FAVOR AND THE DAY OF VENGEANCE OF OUR GOD, TO COMFORT ALL WHO MOURN, AND PROVIDE FOR THOSE WHO GRIEVE IN ZION — TO BESTOW ON THEM A CROWN OF BEAUTY INSTEAD OF ASHES, THE OIL OF JOY INSTEAD OF MOURNING, AND A GARMENT OF PRAISE INSTEAD OF A SPIRIT OF DESPAIR. THEY WILL BE CALLED OAKS OF RIGHTEOUSNESS, A PLANTING OF THE LORD FOR THE DISPLAY OF HIS SPLENDOR. THEY WILL REBUILD THE ANCIENT RUINS AND RESTORE THE PLACES LONG DEVASTATED; THEY WILL RENEW THE RUINED CITIES THAT HAVE BEEN DEVASTATED FOR GENERATIONS. STRANGERS WILL SHEPHERD YOUR FLOCKS; FOREIGNERS WILL WORK YOUR FIELDS AND VINEYARDS. AND YOU WILL BE CALLED PRIESTS OF THE LORD, YOU WILL BE NAMED MINISTERS OF OUR GOD. YOU WILL FEED ON THE WEALTH OF NATIONS, AND IN THEIR RICHES YOU WILL BOAST. INSTEAD OF YOUR SHAME YOU WILL RECEIVE A DOUBLE PORTION, AND INSTEAD OF DISGRACE YOU WILL REJOICE IN YOUR INHERITANCE. AND SO YOU WILL INHERIT A DOUBLE PORTION IN YOUR LAND, AND EVERLASTING JOY WILL BE YOURS.
> ISAIAH 61:1-7

When I read this scripture, all it shouts to me is **hope**. My purpose is to bring hope to those who have lost it. This is a foundational scripture that I stand on that has ushered me into another piece of my spiritual growth and validates my life's purpose and calling. Going through that scripture memorization was so fulfilling to me on many levels. *That was for me!*

There were many other enlightening moments I experienced while I was involved in the Liberty Church community. In the meantime, though, after going through two divorces, and I had finally met my husband that I am with now until the day I die. I had transitioned into a whole new world of entrepreneurism as we decided to start our own business together. Even though there were seasons where I wasn't involved with Liberty Church, due to moving, the lessons always seemed to stay with me. My spiritual growth continued no matter what community I involved myself with. I had such a rich, firm foundation with what I had learned at Liberty, that no matter where I went, I had the discernment and the ability to recognize God and continued to grow. After embarking on the journey of growing our own business, I found my personal growth continually flourishing as I attended all of our unique business events. Later, I returned to Liberty Church, for an even deeper experience of spirituality, but thankfully, some personal growth and development took place during the interim.

CHAPTER 2

Phone Call on the Way
to Warm Springs

On April 4th, 2012, in the early part of my marriage to Pete, I had been listening to a Louise Hay audio, **_You Can Heal Your Life_**. Because I had developed a strong foundation from Liberty Church, I was able to find sound spirituality in almost everything I encountered. From Eckhart Tolle to Louise Hay to Joyce Meyer, I could find spiritual Truth in all of it. As I was listening to Louise Hay that day, I learned about verbally speaking positive affirmations. Earlier that week, I surprisingly lost a job that I had enjoyed for close to a year. That had devastated me because I had just been honored there for achieving great success. I'm certain I was asked to leave because I busted their salary comp plan. The retail establishment that employed me was not looking forward to compensating me for the sales I produced. I had become the top producer in the entire southeast region for an overpriced department store line of luxury cosmetics. Strangely, I had no sales experience. The idea of sales or numbers did not appeal to me at all. I simply invested time and great care into building relationships to create repeat clientele. The numbers created themselves when all the little old ladies wanted to spend money, likely because I lent them a listening ear and a smile. I genuinely cared about them and their lives at a time when possibly no one else offered such attention.

As I stood in front of the mirror, I spoke out positive affirmations for the first time. I still have the list! See below:

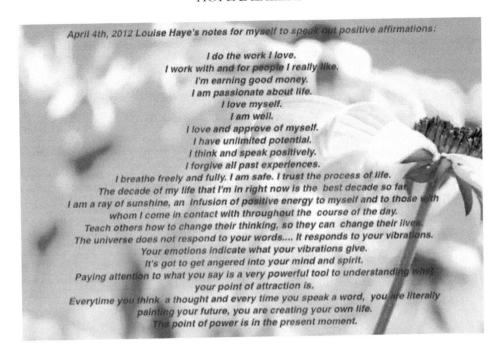

April 4th, 2012 Louise Haye's notes for myself to speak out positive affirmations:

I do the work I love.
I work with and for people I really like.
I'm earning good money.
I am passionate about life.
I love myself.
I am well.
I love and approve of myself.
I have unlimited potential.
I think and speak positively.
I forgive all past experiences.
I breathe freely and fully. I am safe. I trust the process of life.
The decade of my life that I'm in right now is the best decade so far.
I am a ray of sunshine, an infusion of positive energy to myself and to those with
whom I come in contact with throughout the course of the day.
Teach others how to change their thinking, so they can change their lives.
The universe does not respond to your words.... It responds to your vibrations.
Your emotions indicate what your vibrations give.
It's got to get angered into your mind and spirit.
Paying attention to what you say is a very powerful tool to understanding what
your point of attraction is.
Everytime you think a thought and every time you speak a word, you are literally
painting your future, you are creating your own life.
The point of power is in the present moment.

I read these affirmations in my mirror that morning repeatedly. In my heart, all these affirmations fit under my criteria of loving God with all my heart and loving one another (which includes myself), so I was at peace. Part of loving God was the realization that God created me, so I had to learn to love me. At this point, I had been taught many spiritual lessons, but one area I had not yet mastered, was learning to love myself and learning to be completely secure with my self-esteem and my identity. These lessons were just beginning to make themselves known in my life and would fully flourish soon enough.

I continued to recite these affirmations while waiting for Pete to complete a lengthy business call. I was boldly proclaiming out loud, "I do the work I love. I work with and for people I really like. I'm earning good money. I am passionate about life. I love myself." The irony was that I was jobless! What was I going to do? I was seriously unemployed. I just kept reciting the affirmations and allowed my heart to be led by trust, belief, faith, and *hope*.

My husband finally got off the phone and said, "Let's go on an adventure. Let's take the day off and journey down to visit the Little White House in Warm Springs, GA." *Take the day off from what?* I thought. We hopped in the car and started driving in hopes that I would get my mind off of my recently lost job.

During our drive, we received a phone call out of the blue from a previous real estate business associate of Pete's. As the affirmations were still freshly brewing in my mind, I overheard Robb Campbell on the phone with Pete asking him to take a look at a current project he was working on in the travel and lifestyle industry. Pete rolled his eyes and said, "Oh no no, I'm not interested in any projects in the travel industry or any of these side businesses where you have to build networks of customers. I'm in real estate, I've done travel before, and I'm not interested in building another business. Not interested." My ears were perked, and I was totally tuned in to their conversation. I elbowed Pete and said, "Give me the phone!" As my husband dismissed this entire idea, I began conversing with his former business partner, Robb.

I had just made a decision that morning to remain open and receptive. I had just finished stating those affirmations. I'm not stupid, and I'm too spiritual to believe in coincidence. *I just prayed* about my work situation and stated that I was passionate about life! Then within an hour this guy, Robb, calls out of nowhere and starts talking about having fun traveling the world and making money in the process. I was ready to listen. I wanted to travel. I wasn't too sure about the money part as I was no business person. I was a teacher and mom. *I sure did want to travel.* If I could just see the world with my husband and children through travel, then I'm sure God would take care of the money part, because remember, I was no business person. In addition, I was certainly not a sales or marketing person. I could make some great homemade bread from freshly milled grain and teach kids how to read. That was my talent, teaching children and cooking. *I sure did want to travel.*

So, how did this thing work anyway? I wanted to know. I had to know. Did I mention I had the travel bug? Just one problem. No money. *Ahh . . . whatever . . . nothing is impossible with God.* If he wanted me to travel and see the world, He'd work it out for me. I didn't mind staying in cheap hotels or hostels. I just wanted to see the world with my family. I wanted to explore. I wanted to have adventures and create memories and collect some smiles along the way. But wait. We have 6 kids together. Pete has 3, and I have 3. To travel as a family, we are looking at expenses and airfare for 8. Pete had just gone through the big real estate downturn of 2008 and was still trying to recover. Wait . . . reality check; one international flight would break the bank for at least a year! What was I thinking? In spite of reality, I decided that I'm just going to remain open and receptive. I'm going to just roll with this and see what happens. I just prayed for something, and now this really successful guy that did 1 billion dollars in annual sales in real estate is calling us. I'd be a moron not to just find out a little bit more.

Next thing you know, we found ourselves with Robb and his wife Kim in Las Vegas at this huge company event called "United! Living the Dream 2012."

CHAPTER 3

The Church of Tommy Bahama and Flip Flops

*I*s this really a travel company? It didn't seem like it. Who were these people? They were different. I liked being around their energy. It just didn't seem like a serious business event.

Why are people wearing blue jeans and flip flops and Tommy Bahama shirts?

I guess I better go back to my hotel room and change out of my suit skirt and pressed shirt. I thought they said this was a real business?!!

What I discovered very quickly is that we had gotten involved in a personal growth and development company *disguised* as a super fun travel club. The owner didn't even wear a suit! In fact, he seemed more like Walt Disney than Bill Gates. And he never stopped laughing either. I don't remember him speaking a single sentence without this unique little joy-filled laugh. Wow. How interesting. I didn't know entrepreneurism and business looked like this. I watched intently, eyes wide open.

I began to learn that many of the leaders in this community had journeyed through the vortexes of the big-time *personal growth and development* gurus such as Tony Robbins, Jim Rohn, John Maxwell, Zig Ziglar, and Dale Carnegie. The mindsets and functionality of this leadership team appeared surprisingly unlimited. These people were extremely high functioning and well developed in the *personal growth and development* arena. Their thought patterns seemed light years ahead. Being around them was not intimidating though. There was a feeling of joy, and it felt like a fresh breath of life to be around them.

I flashed back to that affirmation I continually recited, *I work for, and with people I really like.* I liked these people. They were reading books from Napoleon Hill, Dale Carnegie, and Earl Nightingale. I thought to myself, *what was the last book I read?* As a schoolteacher, I think it was a Judy Blume book that I read to my class. This experience began the introduction to my personal growth and development company and community that I am still involved with today.

I soon came to discover that there was hope for travel in my life. As of today, 66 vacations later in the past 7 years, I never thought I would be around the world and traveled to as many places as I've traveled to. My kids! I would've never imagined they'd have this many experiences. I found this concept to be an incredible vehicle for the average person, like myself, to take a shot at living a more enriched life designed on **my terms**. I realized that the average person could actually live a VIP lifestyle that I previously assumed belonged only to the rich and famous. I discovered travel experiences that were accessible to the average person. Literally . . . the champagne lifestyle on a beer budget.

In addition to finding hope in my life for travel, I began to discover hope for financial freedom. There was actually **hope** that I didn't have to live life paycheck to paycheck. I could create and design my life in a way that produced financial freedom. I learned about the concept of leverage taught in Robert Kiyosaki's book **_Rich Dad Poor Dad_**. I learned about how to build sustainable wealth through team building and creating a passive income. I attended one of the top high schools, Lassiter High School, in Marietta, GA. I graduated from the prestigious University of Georgia.

Why hadn't I been taught any of these concepts or strategies in school?

I was surrounding myself around the masters of higher thinking and masters in the art of life design. I learned that who I surround myself with is who I will eventually become—choose carefully. If I wanted to be joyful, I must surround myself around those who have mastered joy. If I wanted to have success in any area, I needed to surround myself around those who had undeniable success in that area—*osmosis*.

I was grateful to have received a solid spiritual foundation as that helped me to discern and recognize that these mentors and leaders were not superficially successful. There was some blood, sweat, and tears filled with many lessons on their road to success. For the most part, they exhibited a strong, solid, devoted walk with God. I observed as the owner and the founding members displayed a love for God and a love for one another through their actions. I remember one time the owner of our company did his entire keynote speech on the prayer, *Our Father*. I then began to access and discover a whole new arena in life that was grounded and founded on the same general spiritual philosophies that resided in the core of my heart.

I experienced incredible personal progress achieved by simply choosing two powerful attitudes ever: being coachable and teachable. I learned the wisdom of mentorship and how that carried a strength that was directly correlated to the level of coachability I chose. I didn't necessarily learn these particular skills in the church. Although we learned how to humble ourselves and surrender our egos, I don't remember hearing much on mentorship and being coachable. I heard the message loud and clear in this community. I learned that if I wanted what the average person didn't have, then I would need to do what the average person wouldn't do. I know that God is evidenced in communities of people who love Him, walk with Him, honor Him, and love one another. Whether it's an organized church or a personal growth and development community disguised as a travel club, either way, spiritual growth occurs. I found myself inevitably thriving around all the others with these foundational beliefs and higher functioning mindsets.

CHAPTER 4

Freedom Flavored Juice

I realized there were people in my church community living paycheck to paycheck, working 40 hours a week, who are hardworking, ethical individuals of great character making an honest living. I had been taught this ethic my whole life: go to school, make good grades, get a good job, work 40 hours a week for 40 years so that I could retire on 40% of my earnings—*the 40/40/40 plan*. There was nothing wrong with this plan. Working hard at your job is respectable and honorable by all means. I had just craved something different.

I had a taste for time and money freedom. I had an insatiable desire to design my life on my own terms. If my child was sick at home, I didn't want to ask a supervisor permission to stay home and care for my child who needed my attention. I also didn't want to ask someone permission to use the bathroom. There were times I just wanted to sleep in my bed on a Monday morning until l was **done** sleeping. I didn't want to wake up to the anxiety of a buzzing alarm clock. I wanted to be with my previous dog, Luigi, in his last days of sickness and not worry about how that would affect my paycheck. I wish I had been able to get up and go when my grandmother had a stroke, or when my aunt died. I wanted to be free to have the time to do what I wanted *when I wanted*. I also did not want finances to dictate my decisions on what I could and could not do. I also began to realize that if I didn't find a way to make money while I sleep, I would have to work until the day I die.

I was now aware that I had to create a passive income that would still keep coming in whether I showed up for work or not. I desired to create a legacy that will carry on long after I am gone from this earth. My eyes had now seen that there was *a way* to do this. I witnessed thousands of people from ordinary backgrounds like myself, who were achieving this dream and making it a reality. I now had been spoiled forever with the taste of freedom. Again, to achieve this though, I would need to do something different from what I was taught in school because what I was taught in school wasn't lining up with these new thought patterns and honest desires.

I made my decision, I proceeded to, 1) pay close attention to the training and the lives of those who had the lifestyle I wanted, 2) I stayed excited and surrounded myself around those who were on a similar mission, and 3) I never quit (although many times I sure did feel like quitting on my dreams).

It wasn't but just a couple of years later that I found myself on top of Machu Picchu in Peru realizing that my current reality was more than I could have ever asked for or imagined. The commitment to my dream and the actions taken that lined up with my vision, had paid off. I had a level of freedom I could only have dreamed of before. This time I was able to be there with my dog, Daisy, when she went through her last days. I didn't have to call in to work when my husband had his heart attack. I didn't have to submit a vacation request when I wanted to take a group of young people to build a school in a 3rd world country. I didn't need to fabricate an excuse anymore for when I wanted to be available for my kids or when I wanted to take in a child whose parents had passed. I was totally available to serve God now, and the list goes on. I didn't have to think about the money. That is true financial freedom to me, to do what I genuinely want and need to do without thinking about the money. In fact, when I would check out from this new "work" to do "life," my money would still come in whether I "worked" or not. This was only the beginning. I knew I still had many more levels of freedom to reach, but this taste is enough to keep the hope alive. The juice is definitely worth the squeeze. I like this juice—*freedom flavored juice.*

CHAPTER 5

God and Money: Inner Peace Outer Abundance—Can I have BOTH?

I really learned and experienced that there is hope for financial freedom. I think back to my church teachings. They really did not teach wealth-building or passive income as a type of financial freedom in the church, and I now understand why. I remember doing a Dave Ramsey course on Financial Peace and that was amazing. The course did teach the wisdom of living below your means and not above your means, and not being a slave to your debtors, and being debt-free. I honestly saw a handful of debt-free people in the church who were happy, and they had their freedom—awesome. They seemed to be few and far between in the church community.

I also witnessed many people striving to become debt-free; yet, they seemed to have no joy in the journey. It appeared they were so rigid with their finances that there was no breathing room to have just a little fun and enjoy life. Some people think they can wait to go on vacation until they are 60 years old. They might be slower, and their knees might not work as well by then, but hey, at least their house will be paid off and they're debt-free. They could see the world scooting around in a wheelchair lugging an oxygen tank. There are those who wait for that time in their lives. *Not for me!* For me, I want to enjoy every moment that I can, and if I was called to fully enjoy every moment that I can, but didn't have the money for that, then I would absolutely have to find a way to raise my income level to match the joys and the adventures that I wanted to experience with creating memories and collecting smiles traveling with our

kids. I've seen many people leave this world too early. Tomorrow is not promised."—
Carpe Diem

Even more so, I wanted to have more money to have the ability to give greatly, and to complete large humanitarian projects in the name of Love, in service to God. Money never excited me. I was never into the material world, whatsoever. I remember growing up with plenty of money when I was a child. However, money seemed to disgust me.

I equated money with being attached to lots of meaningless materialistic crap combined with countless arguments. I witnessed people having plenty of money arguing over what to do with the abundance they were blessed with. I didn't like any of it. In my early years, I had wished to be a poor happy hippy.

There came a time when my father chose to leave the restaurant scene where all the money was made. Although we had everything money could buy, we did not have the time or attention of our dad. He was always busy running his prestigious restaurant outside of Utica, NY—***The Aylesbury Inn***. The classiest restaurant around in the 1970s and '80s. We would often join him for dinner. We'd play in the lounge and munch on the large barrels of popcorn. Playing backgammon and drinking our *"Shirley*

Temples" at the bar during slower times was always fun. I even remember meeting Chuck Mangione and some other popular musicians as they'd pass through the fancy *discotheque*. When my father chose to leave the restaurant, we were overjoyed. The Mercedes, Cadillacs, Audis, Porsches, all went away. I found myself having the time of my life riding in my dad's old orange Vega with him. I didn't mind that the floorboards were rusted through. It was fun to peel off scrapings of the orange paint that were falling off the car. And who needed electric push button windows anyways? The roll-up windows were cool! I smiled from ear to ear as my dad and I drove by his friends' homes and threw M-80's in their front yards. We scared the living daylights out of them.

On Sunday mornings, I'd wake up while it was still dark outside, 15 degrees below zero, just to jump in the car and deliver the newspapers with my dad. Life was great when we were poor. My parents didn't find poverty as enjoyable as I did, so it didn't last very long. At 13 years old, my parents decided we would leave New York and move to Atlanta, GA where my father had found more lucrative opportunities. That was hard for me to move so far away. Grandma was also so scared for us three girls, that she had to come with us to make sure we would be ok. Everything seemed to be driven by money, money, money. *Why did we need money anyway?*

One of my mentors, Kim Campbell, taught me of this harmonic balance. Kim is an extremely successful entrepreneur and an international bestselling author of the book **_Inner Peace Outer Abundance_**. The core belief behind this global movement she founded, is that God definitely wants us to have our inner peace and our priorities in check. Love, joy, peace, patience, kindness, goodness, faithfulness, gentleness, self-control—loving God with all our heart and loving one another. Materialism has no part in any of that. *However*, at the same time, there's this marvelous symphonic balance between inner peace and the outer abundance.

There were some big things that I knew God had called me to do. How was I going to do those things if I was broke without the financial resources that it required to get those done? I wasn't greedy for money ever, and still have no interest in being greedy for money, but what I really desired was to do all that God wanted me to do to fulfill his purposes. With my particular calling, I knew that it would require a lot of money.

CHAPTER 6

The Right Place at the Right Time to Cultivate Passions and Purpose

I found myself in the right place at the right time and in the right industry with our personal growth development community *that was disguised as a travel club*. The adventure travel was just the fun part, but the timing of this industry created a freedom aspect that led to a fulfillment that I experienced in multiple ways.

Finally, I didn't have to worry about showing up at a job where I was trading most of my time for money to pay my bills, ultimately building someone else's dream. I finally created a residual income allowing me the time and finances to follow the passions that God put in my heart and created me for. Bringing hope to others was a passion I've had ever since I could remember. With my new found freedom, I was able to create my nonprofit, HopeDealers Worldwide. Of course, the nonprofit was inspired as a reaction to my son's journey, but even if I had not experienced that rocky road, I still would be in some sort of nonprofit, mission or ministry that serves others. That's where I personally find tremendous fulfillment.

Dealing hope is my passion. I'm certain that's what God created me to do in all kinds of imaginable ways. For me, a 40-hour a week job would have taken away my time from developing what I was truly passionate about and designed for. All I wanted to do was to create all sorts of things and to also co-create with others. I found regular jobs to be distracting to my creativity and co-creativity. I can only speak for myself, but maybe there is something in what I'm saying that resonates and stirs up some hope in others.

Again, I know some people are called to work 40-hours a week, and I respect and honor them for following their calling; we're all called to something different.

I do tend to believe that there are many people in this world that if time and money were not an issue, they would be doing something completely different in their lives instead of showing up at their current job. It's a blessing to have the freedom to cultivate your passion and allow your creativity to be fully expressed. Then finding yourself co-creating with others, which is even more marvelous. When you get to spend your time operating in that which you are passionate about, it is usually the hardest yet most enjoyable and fulfilling work you'd ever imagine. We'd likely be much healthier and happier people. We'd be more well-developed, well rounded, and wholesome in every area of our lives if we all could cultivate, create, and co-create according to our passions that are in our heart that we were created for. When people really find their passion, their passion will naturally make them money. For me, I learned how to create a residual income, so the money part was taken care of so that I could have the freedom to cultivate my passions. It was a whole new realm that I came into. I am grateful to have been taught by the best of the bests in my personal growth and development community of exactly how to do that.

I understand why this philosophy isn't promoted greatly in church communities. It could be a conflicting message taught in the church, because what about the people who are called to work the 40-hour a week job and they really enjoy that because that's what they're supposed to do? That's their purpose, and they are genuinely fulfilled. You can't deter someone from that. I think the church has a responsibility to connect with everyone, and maybe for those that feel that they're called to something different and out of the ordinary like I was, then they should just add that in their lives in addition to their church community.

CHAPTER 7

The Riviera Maya Experience

One concept I've learned to grasp is that our challenges are just opportunities. Challenges are carefully designed opportunities intended for us to grow. Part of my journey has been the realization that things don't happen to me, they happen for me. I began to learn that everything is meant and happens for a reason. Everything has its purpose. All things work together for a greater purpose—to refine us or to prepare us.

I had much potential for growth in the area of security, self-esteem, and identity. This area was largely influenced over the years through several mentors, but nothing solidified my lessons in this area as much as one particular experience. The whole family, all eight of us, had finally come together to experience our first international trip at an all-inclusive resort in the Riviera Maya, outside of Cancun in Mexico. I experienced a situation that really bothered me. My feelings were deeply hurt. I was so shaken almost more than any time I can ever remember. I realized that back then, my security in myself, my self-esteem, and my identity was not as solidly rooted as it needed to be. I was so upset, hurt, and irritated with the actions instigated by one of our kids, that I ended up going to a counselor for a year after that trip until I got everything sorted out. I worked weekly with Sylina, one of the most amazing life coaches ever!

She taught me about the importance of practicing forgiveness. We had always learned in church to forgive one another, but it was still somewhat of a new concept for me to *actually practice* forgiving, blessing, and *then* sending love to others that we felt had offended us!

A pivotal lesson she shared with me was the practice of forgiving myself first. Anything from the past, anything I had done that was less than perfect, I was to embrace, accept, learn from, and forgive myself—all of it. This whole process of learning to forgive myself of anything that I've ever done in my entire life up to this point materialized into a tremendous experience of freedom. I learned again that the past does not determine my future. I also learned to embrace all negative experiences in the past and to perceive them as lessons. Therefore, I place myself in a position of having no regrets, whatsoever.

I learned to practice taking the crappiest of experiences and looking at them through a different set of lenses. No matter how crappy or how hurtful that Riviera Maya experience was, I began practicing turning it around by looking for the lesson in it. I can embrace it, accept it, and be okay with it, then leave it in the past and move on. I learned to affirm the experience by professing, "Well, from here forward I've learned a better way in this situation. I have no regrets. I thank God for that experience that helped me to be the better person that I am now. That was really awesome to have experienced that."

CHAPTER 8

The Armor of God, The Gift of Prophecy, and The Mantra

Shortly after the Riviera Maya Escapade and the year of counseling and coaching, I came across a book that my pastor, John Fichtner, from Liberty Church wrote, called **_Prayers Answered Immediately_**. The book was really about The Armor of God, and how I can apply each piece of armor that is referred to in the Book of Ephesians to everyday living, survival, and conflict. This book gave me hope! The entire system in this book helped me feel confidently equipped for overcoming the daily attacks of life. Reading about the breastplate of righteousness completely solidified my entire sense of security. All insecurity I had ever experienced previously was gone after I understood and applied that piece of armor. My identity became solely found in God and how God views me. That was a pivotal life-changing moment in my journey that ushered in more freedom.

Also during this time, I participated in a class about prophecy at Liberty Church, where I learned the true meaning and the true use of prophecy. I learned that in this day and time, prophecy is intended for the sole purpose of edifying and building up other people. If I could surrender myself to my higher power, which for me is God, and get myself and my ego out of the way, and if I was genuinely open and receptive, then I could hear what God would say, according to his character in scriptures, in any given situation or about any person. To move into that position, I had to have my full security and identity placed in God. When I am able to set the ego aside and truly find my security and identity in God through Jesus Christ and realize how God views me and God's opinion of me, I can then exercise my ability to prophecy over other people. This means I can look at others and see them the way that God would see them . . . through the eyes of love. I can build people up, encourage them, and edify them in ways as God would use me as his mouthpiece.

This was really an incredible experience to develop my spiritual eye to be able to prophesy and see things in others the way God would see them. God is Love, and so I would look at people through the eyes of Love. To be able to forgive others, I had to have the insecurity issues of the ego wiped away and cleared out and the blockages removed. My security and identity must remain purely and fully in how God sees me. Once I comprehended that truth of how God truly saw me, it evolved into a game changer in every aspect of my life.

This is the massive lesson that brought me to what I call my daily mantra, as mentioned in a previous chapter. Everywhere I go, I'm reminded of my daily mantra. Everywhere you look around my house and office, this picture can be seen. It is my life mission, and it is worthy of being pictured again below:

MISSION:

TO BE AN EFFECTIVE SERVANT LEADER, IT IS ESSENTIAL FOR US TO **REMAIN** IN THE LOVE OF GOD. WE HAVE TO LEARN HOW TO **SEE** PEOPLE THE WAY GOD SEES THEM. THEN, WE NEED TO LEARN HOW TO **SPEAK** TO THEM THE WAY GOD WOULD SPEAK TO THEM. OUR **INTERACTION** WITH PEOPLE SHOULD CAUSE THEM TO UNDERSTAND AND APPRECIATE WHO GOD IS AND WHO HE WANTS TO BE FOR THEM.

To be an effective servant leader, it is essential for us to remain in the love of God. We have to learn how to see people the way God sees them. Then, we need to learn how to speak to them the way God would speak to them. Our interaction with people should cause them to understand and appreciate who God is and who he wants to be for them.

I don't want anyone reading this book to get hung up on the terminology. If the word "God" is not in your terminology, then just replace it with the word "Love." Because it is my personal belief that God is Love, as the scriptures say, then you can literally take this whole mantra and just say:

"To be an effective servant leader, it's essential for us to remain in Love. We have to learn how to see people the way Love sees them, through the eyes of Love. Then we need to learn how to speak to people the way that Love would speak to them, in loving ways.

Our interaction with people should cause them to understand and appreciate who the author of Love is and who He wants to be for them".

This absolutely revolutionized who I am and how I began to carry myself from that day forward. Every day, I recite my mission, as this is what I choose to live by. It's the passion in my heart.

CHAPTER 9

Copycatting and the Value of Mentorship

I truly thrived and grew so much in my *"personal growth and development disguised as a travel club"* community and continue to do so. The journey is far from being complete. There are still so many people more successful than me that I continue to learn from. If I want the success and lifestyle that I see in other people, *truly successful— not a façade*, then I find others that have success in that area that I want to achieve— marriage, business, parenting, health, etc. Respectfully, I watch them, I listen to them, I study them, everything short of stalking them. Those who have gone before me in that area, I've learned to do exactly what they do until I've achieved that success.

Shortly after first learning the concept "if you do everything that your mentor does, you'll have what your mentor has," I was eating at a restaurant with Kim Campbell. After she placed her order from the menu, the server came to me and said, "What will you be ordering?" I replied, "The same exact what she's eating." I took this concept literally. What she ordered, I ordered. What she ate, I ate. What she did, I did, because I wanted what she had. I then remember being at this Super Bowl party in Deer Valley, Utah. We were on a ski trip with the founder and the owner of our company, Chief Visionary Officer Wayne Nugent. He had secured a condo at the resort to have a Super Bowl party so that we could all watch the Super Bowl together. At the party, I ran into a very successful business partner, Jay Payso. I said to him, "So, Jay, who are you rooting for to win the Super Bowl?" and he turned around and looked at Wayne and said, "Whoever he's rooting for—whoever he wants to win, I want to win." Wayne is the mentor of us all. That stuck with me very profoundly. Someone who's made millions of dollars, someone who's extremely financially successful in his personal growth and development and his entrepreneur career, Jay Payso—he didn't even think to say which team he was rooting for in the Super Bowl, or who he wanted to win. He just immediately turned and said, "Whoever he's rooting for," and pointed to Wayne. I began to see this pattern over and over with people who have this level of financial freedom. They do what their mentors do without even thinking twice about it, without questioning. If you want to be successful, you have to do what other successful people have done before you.

That whole new concept of mentorship became a way of life for me. There was *hope* for this schoolteacher and mom! I began to blossom as an entrepreneur and continue to practice the power of mentorship to this day and for life.

CHAPTER 10

Eye Openers from
the Billion Dollar Couple

I've learned some life-changing lessons from my "travel" community. My first mentors, Robb and Kim Campbell, made an incredible impact on my life. Robb was committed to mentoring us from the beginning. He taught us about the concept of leverage and building systems to create wealth. He showed us how to make money and build teams globally. Robb and Kim created one *billion* dollars in annual sales in real estate and are still crushing it in real estate to this day with Pete. Robb uses these same team building concepts in our travel company also. They are crushing it in multiple industries, in both real estate and travel!

Robb taught us that we didn't have to make money just in our own timezone. We could create leverage from the efforts of others just by knowing someone who could lead and build their own team with us over in Iceland, Hong Kong, South Africa, Australia, or any country or continent for that matter. He'd say, "You see Nadine, while we are sleeping, they are awake in *their* timezone making money that all contributes to the growth of our organization." He taught us that when we go to bed each night, we'd wake up in the morning, and figuratively speaking, there was more money in our account than when we went to bed the night before. *Hence, making money while we sleep.* He taught me how to build teams globally and make money around the world. He opened my eyes to the concept that not only is generating money *not* limited to our timezone, but it is certainly *not* limited to trading our time for money either.

Building great teams and systems generated continual money, whether I was around or not.

To become irrelevant to the process was the goal. The money that was created would outlast us and go on from generation to generation. In my case, it could support our nonprofit long after I'm gone. If I'm gone, it doesn't mean my nonprofit has to be gone. My passive income created is intended to last over and over to continue the nonprofit and the same with creating a legacy for my family. Building generational wealth is what Robb taught us. Generation after generation after generation. If I followed a simple system, my children's children's grandchildren could be "retired" for life.

I'm not fond of the word "retired," because I think we all have a project that God has created us to work on. We all have a purpose and a mission, so I don't think we'll ever be retired. We'll always be doing something. Creating generational wealth also means that our generation after us will have the opportunity to do what they want to do. They will have the freedom to do what God has created them for, without having to worry about going to a job to earn money to survive. I'm so thankful that Robb and Kim taught me the foundations of this age-old concept that was fresh and new to me.

Kim Campbell, as I mentioned earlier, is the founder of the **Inner Peace Outer Abundance** movement. Lots of times, you'll find that money and materialism is highly valued and important in businesses and entrepreneurism where people are generating larger amounts of money. Kim is that person who generates income well above the average person. Actually, she is better described as a ***world dominating tycoon***. Yet, she has no unhealthy connection to the material aspect. I know one of her best friends is a monk, Srinivas, *the traveling monk* as referred to in her book. I'm also honored to call him my friend. This amazing person is a shining example of inner peace balanced beautifully with outer abundance. Inner peace is so important because what good is all that material blessing and all that abundance if you don't have your inner peace? Abundance carries no wealth or value if it is absent of peace.

For me, if I don't have my relationship with God *(loving God, loving one another, serving God and serving others)*, then what's the point of having all that abundance? I could only enjoy materialistic pleasures for so long. I know my true fulfillment doesn't take place until I participate in activities in which I'm serving God by serving others. Kim teaches that simple materialistic pleasures will never fulfill. Yet, simultaneously, Kim creates a tremendous outer abundance. She and Robb are extremely successful in all they do because they understand the deeper principles of creating wealth. They've mastered the concept of leverage through skillfully building global teams, but more importantly, they've mastered the art of inner peace as their foundation.

Looking at the flip side, what's the point of having all this inner peace if you have no outer abundance? What if you are someone who wants to save the world with all these amazing missions and incredible things God created you for, but tragically, you can't stroke the check to buy the food to feed the starving child that you want to help save? All this inner peace is magnificent, but it serves you much better if you have the outer abundance that can fund all the things that you are called to do because you have the inner peace that led you there in the first place.

CHAPTER 11

My Greatest Human Mentor

Kim and Robb introduced me to one of my greatest mentors. This individual has had more influence over my life than any other human being. Jefferson Santos is a best-selling author of the book, ***Higher Life Design***, life mastery trainer, 7 figure entrepreneur, loving husband and super-dad of 2 adorable boys. In addition to building one of the largest networks across the globe, Jefferson along with his wife Megan, have become some of our most admirable friends. He is a stellar example of overall health in all areas of life. Jefferson's entire presence defines the concept of servant leadership. Not only does he walk with God as his foundation, but spiritually, he stays on point and is as solid as a rock. He loves God with all his heart, and he truly is a daily living example of genuinely loving one another. Jefferson is very mindful of his overall health and physical fitness in order to keep his body healthy, so he can perform all that he's called to do. That's an impressive component of well-being that is often not apparent in leadership. Jefferson truly takes it to heart that to be the true servant leader that God has called him to be, he must be in an optimal physical condition so that his health won't hold him back from the massive calling God has commissioned him with.

Everything evidenced in his marriage relationship with Megan is rock solid. Even though we all know there is no perfect marriage, they continue to set an example and higher standard by continually cultivating and applying more and more of what they learn in order to have the best marriage they could imagine.

Jefferson carries that level of excellence in relationships that he has with us as his business partners and his friends. He is loving and gracious and continues to grow, always striving to be a better friend, a better mentor, and a better human being. He exhibits grace and patience not typically seen with people of his stature. Jefferson commits himself to doing the activities that cultivate growth and accountability, forever pursuing personal growth. In his business growth, team-building, and leverage concepts, Jefferson is the founding member of our company and has the largest team in the entire company which continues to expand globally at a ridiculous rate. He also devotes himself to continually evolve in the area of mindset training and brain health. Overall, one of the most well-rounded people, not perfect because nobody's perfect, but definitely one of the healthiest, well-rounded role model I have ever met.

His best-selling book, **_Higher Life Design_**, exemplified to me a balance in all aspects of living a higher life design, and taught me how I could create that for myself. It laid out guidance for how I can shoot for my greatest potential in all of those areas that were previously mentioned. It also taught me that you never fully reach your highest potential, but that you just continue to learn and grow throughout your entire life.

CHAPTER 12

The Master in The Art of Living

If there could be anyone I know who is more personally developed than Jefferson Santos, it would be Wayne Nugent, the founder, owner, and Chief Visionary Officer of our company. Of course, he's Jefferson's mentor. Wayne is like a reincarnated version of Walt Disney. He has this completely out of the box visionary mind that operates at the highest joy level imaginable. He's simply amazing. Because Wayne has such massively innovative dreams and visions, it is incredible to witness him as he wisely delegates other necessary experts to execute those visions for him because Wayne just functions light years ahead of his time. I'm sure he figures you've got to have someone *down here on earth* to usher the logistics into reality. His foundation and his walk with God are evidenced in all that he does. After recently spending time with his amazing mother, Lydia, I can see where this strong influence was initiated from. I had mentioned earlier that at one corporate event at the Dallas Cowboys Stadium, his entire keynote consisted of all slides of the Our Father prayer. That is what he humbly, yet confidently spoke about. He carries this amazing ability to not offend others who may have a different faith; yet lovingly welcomes all faiths and makes all feel inclusive and welcome while not compromising the faith and foundation his company is built upon—God which is *love*. He refers to the book ***As a Man Thinketh***, by Napoleon Hill as if it's tattooed in his brain. I'll often hear him say, "As a man thinketh, so he is," and he truly takes that to heart.

Wayne is a Master in the art of living. There is a poem written where it implies that someone who has mastered the art of living truly has no differentiation between his work and his play. It's all one and the same, and truly that's what he's taught us all. Our passions become energizing, and they become our "work," but it's also our play because we enjoy our passions so much. He truly is The Master in the art of living greater than any human I've ever known.

Again, there is no one perfect human being on this Earth. Even the greatest of humans are still human. But I know that Wayne knows the One who is perfect, and that's where God's beauty is displayed.

A story came into my heart instantly after watching the movie, **_The Greatest Showman_**. I've now watched it more than a dozen times with my family and friends from all my different communities. I sang the songs in my car and recited the story over and over in my head for at least a year. It is such a profound movie that occurred very specifically at the timeliest moment in our company as we experienced a time of _unique growth_ that didn't feel like or look like growth at all. It was more of a time of pruning and purging and weeding out. A collective serious evaluation and refining of our hearts occurred as a community. There was a great sifting, sorting, and separation of the sheep from the goats. The ground was shaken, and those who paid attention and built a firm foundation survived the purge. Those who built their foundation on loose sand, jumped ship when the storms got rough. The most masterful deception overtook some who were considered the wisest.

Basically, crap was flying in every direction imaginable.

However, in the movie, I truly envisioned the greatest showman as the owner and founder of our company, Wayne. I'm going to let that thought usher us into our next chapter. What I learned through this one particular year of struggle that we *all* experienced, collectively brought us to a level where we came out refined, unified, and stronger than ever shining like diamonds.

The Greatest Showman— A Story of Historical Significance to be Shared for Generations to Come

Once upon a time, there was a man who was an incredible dreamer and visionary. This man believed with his whole heart and soul in a million dreams and visions. One day, they actually came to fruition and manifested into reality. He developed what is currently known as the modern-day Circus.

P.T. Barnum created an innovative and disruptive mode of entertainment. His creation was something different, engaging, and captivating. He started with animals and large beasts from all over. After listening to the voice of his child, he incorporated oddities into his acts. Oddities were people with exceptional attributes, giftings, and appearances. Some even dared to call them "freaks." P.T. Barnum allied with those "freaks" and together they co-created the Greatest Show on Earth that attracted customers from all over the nation.

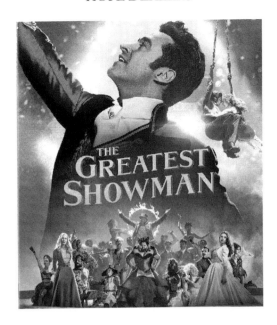

Together, they not only changed the face of the entire entertainment industry, they downright disrupted the entire industry. It was clearly game changing with all that this new Circus idea had to offer, and no one was doing anything like it. They not only had little to no competition, but they were blessed with this blue ocean strategy. Of course, there were those who were just too cool for this innovative, out of the box mode of entertainment, and they continued to attend the ballets and operas. Others tried to copy and imitate what P.T. Barnum created, but with no success.

Then, there were the straight-out haters who booed the whole operation chalking it off as just a scam. Soon enough, the circus grew to be a very successful organization and attracted customers from all over, especially more exceptional performers that became part of the show. Most of the performers didn't necessarily conform to society before, but at the circus, they finally found their home. In P.T. Barnum's world, they fit right into this fun and adventurous culture that materialized into reality from his dreams.

Everything was going exceptionally well. Sales were through the roof! Record breaking sales month after month after month! The show was just simply the Greatest Show on Earth. There clearly was no other deal that could even compare. Then one day, a beautiful Opera Singer from Europe named, Jenny Lind, came into P.T. Barnum's world. Absolutely nothing could compare to her exquisite talent. She offered what was to be an extremely lucrative and successful addition to P.T. Barnum's already successful act. But she offered more. More, more, more! She was the classiest and most elegant of all opera singers with all the bells and whistles. P.T. Barnum knew that this would bring even greater profits to the company and the exponential wealth could be shared with all the performers in this magnificent world he created.

P.T. Barnum by no means was a greedy man. His heart was so large, and he simply wanted to change all the lives of those in his Circus and create great prosperity for all to enjoy the freedom that he knew so well. He chose to go on tour with her all around the country and made lots and lots of money. Jenny Lind became undoubtedly the greatest hit across the nation. People were lined up to see her in every city they toured. Jenny Lind, the enchanting opera singer with the voice of a nightingale, proved to be a raving sensation. A Platinum One Hit Wonder!

Now back on the home front, the exceptionally gifted people continued running the circus as usual. While P.T. Barnum was gone on tour, completely captivated and intrigued with his new act, a great tragedy occurred. You see, P.T. Barnum was not really around giving his flagship creation, the circus, his full attention. He was genuinely and innocently distracted by the idea of creating more prosperity to share with all his world through his new glamorous act! As he was looking the other way, into the blinking green light, some fraudulent haters crept in and next thing you know, the circus building burned down.

At one point after assessing the devastation, P.T. Barnum sat down amongst the rubble and devastated ruins with several of his devoted employees, his exceptional performers. He turned around and looked them all in the eye with the greatest humility and love for each one of them, knowing that they were sitting upon the precious remains of what they had worked so hard for several years to co-create. "It's all gone guys. I have no money left to give you. You all might as well go home." One of the exceptional performers looked back at him, obviously speaking for all the others, and proceeded to say, "Aw geez . . . we already knew you were all out of money. We are not here for the money, well maybe a little, but not really. P.T., this is our *family*. No one else has ever given us a family like this before, we've never quite fit into a world like this before, and we're here to stay because this is *home*.

The beautiful part about this story is that the performers could look back and see the blessing in the original building structure burning down because it was necessary for the rebuilding process to begin. If the destruction, then the rebuilding—*the great restoration process*, had not begun, they would have never had the idea to create a circus tent that became their mobile platform all over the nation! Next thing you know, they became the bigger and better Greatest Show on Earth. As previously mentioned, they became known as the modern-day traveling circus—a form of entertainment familiar to every boy and girl in every household across the nation.

What a beautiful story that this unfolded to be. It hit closer to home than I had ever expected. I can look back at this story and realize I'm so thankful to consider myself an oddity, or an exceptional person, who is part of an exceptional family, who has been given this incredible opportunity to be able to co-create with an amazing visionary with a million dreams. And when things seemed destroyed, we all grasped on to **hope** and stuck together as a family and rebuilt our world together. Whether the money was there or not didn't really deep-down matter; well, it did a little, but not that much. Because the connection we share, the sense of belonging to a family, and being part of something bigger than us was enough to satisfy the *pure in heart*. We believe in the vision, and we believe in the man who created the vision, we believe in the vision as a whole, we believe in what the vision is evolving into, and we believe in **us** as a family. The reward for surviving the purge has been a journey of meaningful personal growth. I'm so very thankful and grateful for **all of it**. I embrace the journey along with the lessons from the past that have contributed to who I am today so that I can look forward with a fresh vision and **hope** for what is to come. The End.

CHAPTER 14

The Fiery Latina
and her Fearless Warrior

Dave and Yvette Ulloa are two friends and mentors from my travel community that have had a tremendous influence in my life. They partnered with Tony Robbins as platinum partners and went through his Mastery University. They are also Master Practitioners of Neuro Linguistic Programming and are Certified Relationship teachers through Allison Armstrong's Relationship Mastery Program. Early on in our time in our personal growth and development company, Dave and Yvette created two life-changing trips related to multiple aspects of health and fitness. These amazing trips they created, brought our travel community to a whole different level of personal growth and development.

The concepts I learned of unconditional love and non-judgmentalism solidified the deep lessons I had learned originally at Liberty Church. Dave and Yvette inspired me to find what I was passionate about and finding my purpose. They helped me identify many of my limitations and then taught me how to experience breakthroughs from that limited thinking. I'll never forget one of my dear friends in our travel community, Captain Roy Woods. Today he is like a brother to me. I witnessed Dave guide Roy through a massive breakthrough after he released and processed through a tragic occurrence in his life. That trip reinforced my faith and belief that I too can reach beyond my limitations and have massive breakthroughs.

There are many stories of tremendous determination and pushing beyond the limits that I can recall experiencing in my life up to this day—pushing beyond what the average mindset would not do, to have what the average mindset would not have. Even with the smaller instances, such as the story in the previous section of Stefan at the airport. There are so many instances in my life that Dave and Yvette and other mentors have taught me about breaking through and eliminating our limitations and showing us the possibility of doing whatever our mind conceived as long as our intentions were pure.

Yvette's teachings about forgiveness, blessing others who we feel have hurt us, and then releasing them in love made a huge impact on my life. Forgive, bless, release, then send love to them, is a pattern I learned that opened up a deeper level of personal freedom. The foundation of all these principles reminds me of the example in the Bible when Jesus is on the cross, looks at the thief next to him, and says, "Father, forgive him. He does not know what he does." What an impactful lesson.

Dave and Yvette also trained my mindset to believe that I didn't have problems or bad situations in life, nor did I have bad circumstances. Instead, I learned that I have challenges, and all of these challenges are created in my life as opportunities to learn something, experience something, or to grow through something. It was solidified at that point; *my challenges are now viewed as my opportunities*. That's when I fully accepted that bad things in life don't happen TO me. They happen FOR me. This created a whole different mindset that brought extreme liberation and peace, especially as I was dealing with my son and his addiction issues. *This didn't happen to me. This happened for me.* So far, the many opportunities that have come from my son's addiction experience have been amazing, including the creation of our nonprofit. I know we've only touched the tip of the iceberg. I believe my son will have more fruit in his life that will grow from his struggle and our struggle as we worked through it together.

Mindset shift: the challenges and struggles are opportunities.
Things don't happen TO me—They happen FOR me.

Dave and Yvette also taught that we had two choices about the people we surrounded ourselves with. If I was going to expect my mindset to function on a higher level than it was functioning on before, then I need to surround myself with those who were like-minded in attitude. The choices were to either 1) CHANGE MY FRIENDS, OR 2) CHANGE MY FRIENDS. Lol. Exactly. I got the point. Dave Ulloa states it very clearly—you either have to learn to change your friends or change your friends. Pick one. That was pretty profound. I also want to point out that I don't compare myself to other people. I only compare to myself. I don't want to say that I'm better than other people by any means whatsoever. Not at all. There's so much we all can learn from *each other*. The comparison is only to myself; where I was, where I am, and where am I climbing towards in MY own personal growth.

As a result of immersing myself in their intense weekends of mentorship, my perspective shifted. I began to discover my purpose, found myself creating and co-creating with no limitations, and experienced more frequent breakthroughs. I learned to forgive. I learned to bless others. I learned that my challenges are really just opportunities, and I learned to change my friends OR change my friends.

These combined lessons gave me inspiration and confidence to create my own special trip within our travel community. While Dave and Yvette were working on another chapter in their life story during that time, there was a group of us that really wanted to keep these health and fitness themed trips going. I picked up the torch and carried the flame together with the other ladies from the group. I created The Ladies Health and Fitness DreamTrip in Denver/Boulder, Colorado. We would all agree it was legendary. I still maintain close relationships with the ladies who participated in that trip with me to this day.

It's SAFE for you to unleash your inner light, strength, spiritual gifts, and beautiful God-given healing POWER!

Ladies Dream Trip 2015

A few years later, Dave Ulloa created a Warrior's Code trip in our travel community for the guys. My husband's participation in that trip was yet another amazingly unique experience that made a monumental effect in his personal growth. We look forward to one day soon, Dave and Yvette using their relationship certification to create couples' trips that we are eager to participate in. We're just so thankful for Dave and Yvette Ulloa. They've influenced our lives much more than they will ever know. During the editing of this book, they brought us a very special gift all the way from Brazil! Maya, our adorable tan redbone coon hound, is a very special new addition to our family and we are forever grateful for our new family member.

CHAPTER 15

Mr. Clean
and the Prophetic Message

Another person who has greatly influenced my personal growth is Dr. David Pietsch. This large baldheaded "Mr. Clean" looking guy is really a softy with a close and committed relationship with God. He helped me really absorb the concept of the *ultimate sovereignty* of God—the certainty that God is in control and that God still sits on the throne. This concept of sovereignty that God is totally in control, has become solidly ingrained in my mind and in my heart, bringing me to another level of freedom. This is a bold teaching, that God has a greater purpose for everything and that we don't always necessarily understand why things happen. We just don't need to understand. I simply need to trust in the sovereignty of God. I've always been taught this concept, but it was something about the way that Pietsch delivered this message that finally sunk in.

On a side note, not understanding why bad things happen or not understanding why anything happens is a common question in society. That's normally the first question people ask when tragedy occurs. I've quit trying to answer this question as there are no words that can clarify this mystery as well as the book and movie, **_The Shack_** by William P. Young. I promise you, if you watch that movie or read that book, it will absolutely obliterate your need to understand why bad things happen. You will gain a deeper understanding of the sovereignty of God.

One last noted teaching from David Pietsch that was more significant than he probably even realized, occurred at the Dallas Cowboys Stadium, at the same event where our owner and founder, Wayne, delivered his keynote of the Our Father. Our company and community were in the midst of a thriving season. From the stage, David Pietsch delivered a very prophetic message that was exquisitely timely. The training he delivered was not your normal business or personal growth and development message. *But—neither was the Our Father.* David shared a message about how important it is to get your financial house in order. He shared straight from **_The Book of Proverbs_**, the wisdom from the Bible that taught us all if we are to be a higher functioning person than the person we were before, it would be necessary for us to get our finances in order. He firmly advised to make sure we consider having a minimum of six months in savings. Again, *he repeated,* at least six months solid in savings and establish serious financial health before we consider blowing money on these big fun things that a lot of people in our community could finally afford. Many people in our community were beginning to generate some newly found wealth. David cautioned not to be spending money on all these fancy cars and all these material possessions unless our financial house is in order first.

Pietsch was prophetically sharing this message to us. It's as if God was faithfully preparing us to make sure that we were financially solid, just *in case* a challenge was to come. Exactly 6 months later, the storm hit our company touching us all in one way or another. It was a temporary yet necessary struggle in our company. In reference to the Greatest Showman chapter, my perspective is that this challenge ended up being an opportunity we all came to embrace. It made us all stronger and more unified than ever! Any other company would not have survived; yet, **we did**. I thank God for that. But it's not like we hit a hard time for that one short year without warning. I just don't even know if many people realize that this prophetic message was given. It was evident that God loves us so much and is so good to us that we received the warning well ahead of time before the storm blew in. Whether Pietsch realized it or not, God used him to deliver a message that allowed those who **paid attention** to prepare adequately. Thankfully, Pete and I listened 6 months prior and we were prepared. The storm wasn't comfortable to me, yet we survived and came out stronger. Many were not prepared, and their level of discomfort was much greater. Again, in some ways, the reaction to this challenge separated the boys from the men. In the end, God showed himself sovereign, and everything happened just the way it was supposed to happen for the greater good.

CHAPTER 16

Pahrump Valley Winery

I met Dwight and Fadia Hanson along with another couple, John and Cindy Marshall, on one of our first travel adventures. Dwight and Fadia had a powerful impact on us from the very first time we met them. It was very early on in our travel company when we all traveled together to a winery out in the desert of Nevada. I remember Dwight and Fadia coming across as the most genuine, down-to-earth, delightful people to be around. As we were all comfortably conversing with one another, I remember saying, "Well, how long have you been with this company?" Fadia responded, "Well, my husband, he's one of the founding members." I thought, *Oh, my goodness. These guys are hanging with us and they are totally real, cool, and down-to-earth. They feel as familiar as family, but at the same time, they are one of the "big guys," one of the founding members.* I was really impressed. That made a powerful statement to me that people who had all this notoriety and status in our community didn't feel the need to be higher than and above the rest of us. What became immediately apparent about the leadership in this company is that they are family, and we could all congregate with each other comfortably regardless of status within the company. I respect that many had gone before us and paved the way to success in our industry. They've done a lot of the hard work to make our business building easier, but they don't set themselves above us. It made a huge impact on me how humble they carried themselves and how familiar they were with us. The culture created was comfortable, inviting, and felt like family.

On that same adventure is where we met two heroes of **hope**, John and Cindy Marshall. Everyone we met was new to us at that time. John was a retired U.S. Navy Captain, and Cindy was his lovely military wife. They were enjoying the tremendous benefits of being members of this community just as we were. We were absolutely delighted by their presence as we all sat at the same dinner table. John had us continually laughing and displayed one of the most positive mindsets and joyful countenances you could ever imagine. Continually, he would be smiling, laughing, and socializing. As we were completely immersed in the pleasure of their company, for just a moment, John proceeded to pull off a baseball cap that he had been wearing. I noticed a big huge bandage across his head. I comfortably asked, "My goodness, what happened?" He responded without hesitation, "Oh, it's a terminal brain disease. Doctors gave me only a few weeks to live three years ago and here I still am!"

My husband and I looked at each other and our jaws dropped as John smiled from ear to ear. We were both thinking, *This man is dying of cancer. He's terminal and he is sitting here living life to the fullest on a winery trip with us, boisterously laughing, energetically positive, with a joy level higher than the Empire State Building.* There are no words for the depth of the impact that made on both of us. What an incredible man, to say the least. A pillar of **hope** and strength. At each event after that, we made sure we sat right beside them. *I wanted more of what they had.* John passed away approximately two years after that unforgettable trip. To this day, Cindy still remains one of my closest friends. Every time I'm in the

Dallas-Fort Worth area, I always get together with her, we continue to travel the world together, attend all our community events together still seated right beside each other. John's outlook, his attitude, his unlimited belief, his genuine *hope*, his whole demeanor, was a big reason that he ended up living several years beyond the doctors sentencing. He proved to me the power of a healthy mindset and unwavering faith as he also had a close relationship with God. I drew especially close to John and Cindy as they both loved God with all their heart and they loved one another. Simply amazing human beings. I wonder if they'll ever know how much influence they've had in my life.

CHAPTER 17

The Wise Farmer

Byron Schrag is a "countryman" and knows quite a bit about farming. He taught me how to conduct myself in business as a farmer does. This analogy greatly influenced my business perspective. Byron shared that when the farmer plants the seeds in the ground, he's not emotionally attached to the seeds that he's planting, nor is he even emotionally attached to the act of planting. He simply delivers the seeds, plants the seeds, and realizes that you really don't know until much later if they actually took root, or if they are even going to grow into a vibrant plant. You take your chances, and you spread all your seed. He taught me that I could not emotionally attach to prospecting customers for our business. We just spread the information, get it all out there, don't look one way or the other, or even care if they take or not. We just do our job and plant our seeds. We find out later if they actually take root or if our customers actually become fruitful members of our organization. Learning this concept of emotionally detaching from our business efforts was extremely liberating, transforming the act of sharing our product into a peaceful and pleasant experience.

In my beginning years of an entrepreneur, I was emotionally concerned whether my prospects were going to say yes or no to becoming a customer. I feared the rejected feeling of the word "no." I've learned that a successful business builder has no emotional attachment whatsoever to their prospect, whether they make a sale or not does not matter. There are zero emotions attached. Another mentor of mine, Eric Gryzbowski, displayed it clearly. In order to emotionally detach from the idea of converting an exposure into a sale, I just say in my mind, "Some will, some won't, so what, who cares?"

Continuing with the planting analogy, Byron taught me that when a farmer is planting, his eyes remain looking forward, planting his rows in straight lines focused ahead. The rows don't zigzag or look to the side or back and forth. In business, this encouraged me greatly to keep my mind straight forward focused, not being deterred by the multitude of distractions on the side. I simply learned to just get up, plant my seeds, and stay focused. I go straight forward ahead just as the farmer plants his crops. Sure enough, that simple principle applied in my business yielded me success.

CHAPTER 18

The Author of Familyshipping

Another person who surprisingly influenced me is a man by the name of Darron Walker. Through his persistence and determination, he's achieved remarkable success. Unknowingly, he taught me how to have more grace, understanding, and trust with others concerning my personal business organization. One time, our corporate office sent him to conduct a training in our local market. I actually became frustrated with him because I had invited some very successful professionals to come to this event. Darron's style of training wasn't necessarily in congruence with the "highly refined corporate professional" that my guests were expecting. They were offended and irritated by the raw training style that Darron delivered. My guests walked out of that training. *I was pissed off,* as I felt like I lost some very important, highly successful, professional customers. I was so irate, I wrote a letter to the corporate office about, Darron's style, "His training style is not conducive to the more refined professional." I learned that the "highly refined professional" that appeared to have it all together wasn't necessarily open-minded to the fact that there are all different styles out there. A wise business person remains open-minded to all the different styles, including the ones that are not perceived to be as "highly refined" as they may be used to.

I also learned lessons about the value of being genuine and real with business relationships. Darron is cool with who he is and confident with the training he delivers. If a person was uncomfortable with a particular style, maybe they could consider looking deeper into the business wisdom of being genuine and real. That was an extremely humbling experience and lesson that I learned. I also learned to have grace, understanding, trust, and a tremendous amount of respect for the raw, genuine truth and unique style that Darron has.

I've come to fall in love with a particular term he created. **Familyshipping** is a spin-off of the word *fellowshipping* which would be commonly used in a church setting. Darron created that term called **Familyshipping**. Any time we get together with the people in our personal growth and development community, we are all like family, and so we just call it **familyshipping**. For example, "And here we are all familyshipping around the pool, or here we are familyshipping on the ski slope, or at the beach, or wherever we are in the world." Full credit goes to Darron, but I'm caught using it all the time.

I tie this all to the continual theme of HopeDealers Worldwide. The opposite of addiction is connection. The connection that we have created through the **familyshipping** in our travel community is absolutely amazing. It's not common to see anyone struggling with addiction in our travel community. Could it be because we have such a strong connection? Any time you have a group with a strong sense of belonging to a community, that connection can be a powerful force resulting in the prevention of addiction. If I really consider the opposite of addiction as connection on a deeper level, it's not just connection with one another. The whole objective of us having connection with one another should lead us to a higher level of connection, ultimately, with our higher power, with God himself. It comes down to my spiritual philosophy again. Love God with all your heart and love one another. Have connection with God with all your heart and have connection with one another. It all simply fits together.

CHAPTER 19

Female Empowerment Leaders

April Consulo was elected mayor at a city just outside of Nashville. She was extremely accomplished in multiple areas of her life, and she carries that success into building her business in our personal growth and development community. She taught me how to have backbone and how to persist with an incredible drive while simultaneously being a very loving, caring, nurturing person. This perfectly mixed cocktail of drive, assertiveness, and initiative, while still maintaining that natural character that we both have of being very caring, nurturing people was appealing to me. I began to grow a genuine backbone that I never knew was there.

Sebrena Kelly is a Caribbean princess who leaves a legacy wherever she walks. Sebrena, who was previously named #1 Black Woman Networker in Atlanta, carries herself with a grace and humility that inspires me each day to become a better me.

I've been blessed to develop close friendships with many of my business partners. Both Jackie Brown and Arleen Hughes impress upon me greatly the way they consistently maintain a radiant level of joy. These two ladies operate uniquely in their own way on such a high level of joy, regardless of circumstance. I know they're not perfect; they have life challenges also. But overall, consistently, I can count on them for maintaining that joy level. Their commitment to faith and hope is the catalyst for that joy level. I consciously choose to surround myself with them whenever I can, as I desire to have what they have.

They both are women who have devoted themselves to serving others through consistently offering inspiration and radiant joy to all those around them. Sometimes, when I'm feeling discouraged, I say to myself, *Oh, I need me some Jackie Brown*, and I call up Jackie and I get me some *"Jackie Brown fill up"* finding myself refreshed and filled with life again. Jackie has a solid connection to her Source, God. I could share almost anything with her, knowing that I won't ever get influenced or advised in any way that was not clearly and healthfully facing the path of life. Then there's Arleen; words don't even have to come out of her mouth, she doesn't even have to speak—pure radiance emanates just from her smile and her presence refreshing the driest of souls. These two ladies are true sisters to me that I look up to as shining stars in my life.

Skye Williams, one of my best friends, is a fabulous leader I've guided as she's built her organization. She considers me her mentor, but what I have learned *from her* has been empowering. She experienced disappointment and failure in business building at the beginning of her entrepreneurial quest. Yet, she persevered and raised her level of trust. There were times when she attempted to get to training events and she didn't have the money to get there. What this woman came up with to generate money to travel to events was heroic. Skye would do what nobody else would do to get what nobody else had. During a financial low point, she bought cases of water bottles and stood on the street corner in Houston and sold water bottles until she generated about $700 so that she could get to a training event in Miami. I commend her for her commitment, drive, and courage to do something that nobody else would do. Then I evidenced the ripple effect of her actions when I began to hear of others doing what she did when they first started out in order to scrape up some instant cash. She influenced many.

CHAPTER 20

International Expansion: The League of Extraordinary Gents—The Oaxacan Hotel Slave, The Leader Singer of the First Boys Band and The Real Master P

There are a few people in my personal organization that I have had the honor to be considered their mentor in one way or another. Ironically though, I am the one who has learned from them. My *"hermanito"* from Mexico, Beto Ruiz, is an exceptional leader in our organization. I've had the honor and privilege to work beside and help him create his own organization to become a thriving success. His business has flourished with great strength and comradery. Beto's work effort combined with his faith in God through some of the most difficult times financially and mentally has been extraordinary. Just when it looked like nothing would work out, his faith, commitment, and devotion to the cause was simply remarkable. His work ethic puts me to shame, and I'm his mentor! There are no words for devotion and his commitment to never quit. I could write a book just about all the adventures of obstacles and breakthroughs we've encountered, but I'll save that for him to write. Beto is a true born leader that will always be on top!

Our friend, Marshall Pereira, more commonly known as the "real" Master P is an 8th-degree black belt grandmaster in martial arts. He was my husband's martial arts instructor for years. As we've worked together in helping him create his own organization over the years, he has actually helped us with our global expansion. He travels all over the world and trains others in the martial arts. Everywhere he goes, he meets new customers and invites them to be part of our travel club community. Marshall's devotion, level of commitment, and integrity are inspiring to me and to everyone who knows him.

George Mangrum began the journey in our travel community even before Pete and I did. We have grown to become family in the past decade. In his early years, George was an international pop star and lead singer of the first boys band "7th Avenue." He toured through Europe back in the 1980s. By the time we met him, he had retired the microphone and caught the viral travel bug. We continue to co-create and build our travel community together in Atlanta, GA. My friendship with George continues to be a genuine example of faithfulness, consistency, integrity, honesty, commitment, and devotion to brotherly love and respect towards one another. If the world was full of George's, there would be world peace, respect, and kindness to all. No wars would exist. Just lots of blue signs and sunglasses in every color and style imaginable. George is just one of those guys who is always here for you and just simply makes the world a better place just from his sheer presence.

CHAPTER 21

Fresh Hopedealer
Delivery from Heaven

One of my newer mentors, the CEO of our company, Josh Paine, has made quite an impact in my life in the short time that I've known him. From the moment I heard him speak for the first time, I knew that he must have fallen out of the clouds and came straight from the throne room of God to deal us a serious dose of *hope*. He jumped right in and helped execute into fruition the vision that Wayne had, that truly saved our company's butt during the storm. He grasped our challenge straight in the face and boomeranged into an amazing opportunity. He delivered *hope* with strategy and precision. He not only executed a strategic plan to implement Wayne's vision, but he brought an incredible dose of vitamin B12 to the life and vitality of our company bringing us to a new level of vibrant health. Our company has reached a level of vitality more than I've ever seen in the seven years that I've been part of the community.

Josh Paine is a genuine Hopedealer along with the several I've mentioned so far. They are an integral part of the *Community of Believers* committed to dealing pure **hope.** It was no surprise that shortly after meeting Josh, I discovered how strong and committed his walk with God is. Josh regularly professes his need for God in his life. He has come to be known as a living, walking example of love, **hope**, and a servant leader to all. What a blessing God sent our company when he sent us Josh Paine.

CHAPTER 22

The Importance of Human Connection—Community Groups

I've realized the massive importance of commitment to a community and the importance of human connection. Some people in certain communities use the word "fellowship." Other communities use the term "small group." And then some communities, like our *"personal growth and development disguised as a travel club community,"* uses the term "familyshipping," as I've mentioned in a previous chapter. In order to keep hope alive, I found it imperative to be committed to a group of people. Again, our slogan for our non-profit is:

"The Opposite of Addiction is Connection."

In any church type community I've ever been involved in, I've always made sure that I participated in a small group connecting with one another and serving each other. I've always felt that small group is where *"real"* church took place, much more so than the big church service. That's where connection, supporting, and serving one another takes place.

The Travel Community Group: In my travel community, I've never missed a company training or event. I've consistently stayed committed to that, somewhat like a church. We are a like-minded fun group of individuals who travel the world together and experience great adventures together.

The Hopedealers Community Group: After we returned from our trip to Guatemala, we felt the need to nurture the connections made in our relationships with one another. We didn't want to wait until the next trip to connect again, so we formed a support group which went for a short season. The Hopedealers meetings then took an unexpected transformation into a focused group of people working on their drug and alcohol counseling certification. Currently, we have a class with a group that will be together for two to three years working on a common goal with a common purpose.

It has proven to be a great way to keep a group continually connected.

One of the guys in our group experienced a challenge and went through a very brief relapse. Because of the connection that we formed with this group, we had established a relationship where everyone felt comfortable reaching out to him. Thankfully, he came right back into living a clean and sober life. Of course, it was his own decision to come clean again, but I do believe that the relationships in our group had some influence on his decision because he knew that we were there for him, and he felt supported and loved with no judgment. To this day, our CADC class community continues to thrive and serve a real need in the community and in the lives of others.

Liked by **maniicecile**, **nicoleuli** and **16 others**
skyeisono Connection. Something we all found with each other. I love all of them 🖤
massivehomesuccess Super sweet!
APRIL 3

The Ladies Community Groups: In January of 2017, Victoria Webster, Jackie Brown, Nicole Uliana, Arleen Hughes, Pam Passmore, and Rachel Loyd all journeyed up to the mountains to meet Karen Rayside and an amazing group of women. We got snowed in at Brasstown Valley Resort and experienced a magical all-ladies weekend that was unforgettable.

Each Monday morning, I look forward to my ladies' small group. Busyness had gotten the best of me, and I had not been part of a small group in my church in quite some time. I knew deep down I was missing something. I felt for a long time the urging to become a part of a group just for myself with ladies. All the other groups I participated in were coed which often left me feeling limited. I kept feeling like I needed something just for me, just as a woman, to participate in. I certainly didn't have time in my schedule, and I really didn't want to join a new group, but I could not deny the urging that God was placing on my heart.

In January of 2018, I no longer accepted my excuse of being too busy and established myself in a regular ladies group from Woodstock City Church. I like to joke around and think of this group as the *"housewives of North Atlanta."* There are six of us in our group: Melody Kliment, Tracy Ragsdale, Linda Kascor, Nicole Uliana, Jenny Barger, and me. I'm glad that I was obedient to that urging voice I heard in my heart and surrendered to it. It has evolved into one of the best groups ever. Initially, I had walked into a group of ladies that I did not even know. After a couple of meetings, I invited my friends Nicole and Jenny to join us. In just a short time, we've created a connection and a bond that we all cherish. We meet together every single week, we've gone to the movies together, out to eat together, served in homeless shelters and provided Christmas gifts for the needy together. God knew, I really needed that group and the connections that were established. I really didn't want to take more time out of my schedule, but I trusted the voice of God. As a result, it definitely filled a place in my heart where I am so thankful I surrendered to that urging.

The Family Community Group: I am blessed because I have a family that through the years has been a community group on its own. My parents have now been married for over 50 years and have stayed committed through thick and thin. My parents, my older sister Nicole, and my younger sister Noelle, and I always come together for holidays, birthdays, and anytime mom cooks. They are always there and have proven to be the greatest source of support in my life.

CHAPTER 23

The Boy Who Wore the Orange Costume for 34 Days

Dawson's story: As I continued to develop my life in service to others by getting my mind off myself, different situations and scenarios would just pop up into my world. There is a young man in our community, Dawson Crowe, who has been close friends with my stepson, Phillip, all through their school years. They both became lifelong friends through the special needs program. Unfortunately, both of Dawson's parents had passed away. Dawson had been living with his grandparents who have worked very hard over the years to raise several of their grandkids.

An unfortunate situation happened with Dawson's uncle that ended up landing Dawson in jail for something he simply did not do. At the time Dawson was an 89 pound, 5'2" special needs young man that was arrested and placed in the Cherokee County Adult Detention Center for 34 days without bond. Dawson was able to get an an extremely intelligent and strategic attorney, Jay Wall, who worked pro bono for Dawson. But without a legal guardian, the bond hearings proved unfruitful as he was continually denied bond. No one was able to fulfill the guardian need that Dawson had, so I jumped in and did what I could. I became Dawson's guardian, and on day 34 after holding a protest in front of the courthouse, Dawson was finally granted bond after his 3rd bond hearing. We got his bottom out of that jail and out of what he refers to as the "orange costume." With tears in his eyes, Dawson cried, "Mama Deenie, I don't ever want to wear that orange costume again!"

I brought him into my home and took him under my wing in an attempt to provide a fulfilling and healthy lifestyle for him. He still to this day has no clue why he was arrested and incarcerated. With lack of complete understanding, this experience proved to be very scary for him. He'd often say, "Why did I get in trouble for trying to help Uncle Curtis?" To have an intellectual disability, be falsely accused of felonies, incarcerated, and being assumed guilty until proven innocent, was absolutely a horrific experience for a special needs young man. I was given the honorable opportunity to deal some *hope* and rescue the boy in the orange costume from injustice. I found these escapades of mine, *(as my husband would call them)*, to be extremely fulfilling as I continued to experience a mindset to shift from being served the mindset of living life in service to others.

CHAPTER 24

The Rudy Ruettiger Award

Not long after becoming Dawson's guardian, people in my personal growth and development community nominated me for a very prestigious award, The Rudy Award. This award was given to me by football legend, Daniel "Rudy Ruettiger." Rudy Ruettiger is well known as a college football player for Notre Dame that was the inspiration behind the award-winning movie, **_Rudy_**. It was a great honor to be surprised with this award that was based on character, commitment, contribution, and courage. Ironically, I am not into football at all; yet, this was an award given to me by someone who passionately loved football and was noted for his character, his commitment, his contribution, and his courage.

I was the first recipient of The Rudy Award in my community based on the unexpected votes of my peers. My friends have seen how hard I persisted, and how much I had accomplished in such a short amount of time under less than ideal circumstances. Rudy was and still is of shorter stature and was not the first person to be picked on the football team by any means. Likewise, I was simply a mom and elementary school teacher by training. There was nothing glamorous or highly successful about my trade or occupation; yet somehow, I had found my way into success through continual commitment, determination, perseverance, contribution, character, and courage. As Rudy was the least likely to make that play in the football game against Georgia Tech that one day, I was also least likely to achieve the level of success that I have experienced. I was shocked, honored, and thankful to have been the recipient of this award.

I do not attribute the level of success in my business, in my personal growth and development, and in my spirituality to just coming naturally. Again, I was the least likely to taste success, especially in business. I attribute any and all success to God who gave me the strength and wisdom to maintain a constant commitment, to push and push and push. I still have so much farther to go. I have only touched the tip of the iceberg. I have many more levels to achieve, but where I have come so far, has been atypical for someone with my modest background to have achieved. However, in spite of all the obstacles, I continue to achieve through much commitment, much contribution, much courage, and maintaining the best character I can through the whole process in spite of circumstances.

Surrounded by an incredible Community of Believers, I am a living proof that **hope** can be found for your business and finances. There's hope for your emotions. There's hope for your relationships. There's hope for your spiritual, mental, physical, and personal growth.

SECTION 4

Hope found through Loss and Grief

CHAPTER 1

The Passing of My Daisy Rose

Her Highness, Miss Daisy Rose, was my soul sister, my human angel dog. My precious Yellow Lab, Daisy, may have left my side on Oct 4, 2018, after 13 ½ years of best friendship, but she will never leave my heart. Have you ever experienced having a "soul sister" dog, or have you ever loved anyone that you were connected to so deeply that the loss felt earth-shatteringly devastating? This feeling seemed to be accompanied by the loss of ability to function, or think, or eat, or anything!

I remember being on a cruise just two weeks after Daisy's passing having a conversation with some of our best friends, Del and Arleen Hughes. I inquired, "Have you guys ever had a human angel dog?" Del looked at me strangely with one eyebrow raised, "A what?" After clarifying my question by explaining my special relationship with Daisy in greater depth, it turns out that they do have a really great normal dog. And then, Del recalled that he actually once had a **human cat** named Buddy. They remembered how deeply grieved they were when it was Buddy's time to go to kitty cat heaven. I don't think it really matters what type of loss a person experiences, whether it's the loss of a loved one that is 2 legged or 4-legged, loss is loss and produces grief. This was my first experience of **deep loss**. Daisy was part of almost every aspect of my daily life, we were inseparable, and then, she was no more. Emptiness. Void. Loss of words. No words. Deep blow in the gut. Rock in the heart. Gone. Frozen. Speechless. Functionless. My best friend was gone.

CHAPTER 2

Experiencing Grief: The Great Unknown

I was somewhat confused about this feeling of grief because I had never quite experienced it before on this level. I remember the day after Daisy passed, I was at a business meeting with several entrepreneurs in the area. As I stood up for my turn to speak, I unexpectedly broke down in tears and quietly exited the room. I was surprised at myself! This was not my typical behavior. I prided myself on being calm, cool, and collected. I was somewhat freaked out! Why is it that I cannot conduct myself and function professionally after the loss of my dog? It had been a whole 24 hours since her passing.

Thank God my friend, Deb Carmody, who had just flown in from LA, was at that meeting with me. She graciously just picked up the pieces of my short monologue and flowed right into speaking for me, picking up right where I left off as I sprinted to the restroom to wipe my tears. It was obvious I did not understand at that moment what grief really was. I didn't understand that grief deserves to be respected with some time and some processing. I really thought something was wrong with me for not being able to function the next day. After all, this wasn't a spouse or child, this was a beautiful dog who lived a long, rich, full life. Still didn't matter. Grief is no respecter of persons 2-legged or 4-legged, grief is grief.

A friend of mine from that group who is a counselor, Greg Griffin, called me at home later that afternoon to talk to me about what happened earlier in our business meeting. I realized that in spite of all this personal growth and development, spiritual growth, business growth, mental growth, and emotional growth, I remained clueless about the concept of grief. How did I miss that one? I was so thankful Greg gently walked me through grief. He recommended a book, _**A Grief Observed**_, by C.S. Lewis that was tremendously helpful. The very next day, I had been reading content written by Wendy Van de Poll in a Mastermind group that I belong to. She authored a Pet Bereavement series, _**My Dog is Dying: What Do I Do?**_ and _**My Dog Has Died, What Do I Do?**_ I couldn't have come across this series at a more perfect time as I was freshly experiencing this loss. The titles were spot on because I had come to a standstill, I really didn't know what to do! I just needed someone to guide me through these unchartered waters.

I thank God for providing exactly what I needed at that moment. I wish that every single veterinarian would keep a supply of these books in their clinics to offer to every single human who goes through the loss of their pet. Wendy is a pet loss grief coach. I never even knew those existed! Grief support coaches and groups offer great power, strength, comfort, health, and **hope**. I found great wisdom in allowing someone else to guide and usher me through this dark experience escorting me into the light where hope was found. There is hope in grief. I've now walked through the grief journey in a healthier way than expected, and there is no longer the fear of the unknown.

CHAPTER 3

My 4-Legged Mentor

I can look back and truly appreciate how Daisy was one of the most powerful mentors in my life. Lessons from my Daisy Rose:

1. GRIEF– Daisy taught me that there was hope in loss. She allowed me to experience and journey through grief in a healthy way.

2. DEVOTION– There has never been any living entity, other than God Himself, that has shown more devotion to me than my sweet yellow lab Daisy.

3. UNCONDITIONAL LOVE– No matter who, what, when, where, or why, Daisy loved everybody and everyone no matter what, with no judgment. She was never a respecter of persons, there was no race, color, socio-economic status, smell, or anything that Daisy would discriminate against. She loved everybody unconditionally. When I'd feel like the whole world was against me, I knew Daisy was for me. I could count on her.

4. COMMITMENT– Daisy was fiercely committed to me. She would not leave my side for anything. Many times I'd float around in a little raft on the lake, and she swam and swam and swam relentlessly in circles around my raft. She was committed to protecting me.

5. SERVICE TO OTHERS– Daisy served me in all those areas above unlike any human being ever had. This reminded me of how powerful it is to serve others.

Towards the end of Daisy's life, she could not do all that a yellow lab should have been able to do. During her last year, especially her last couple of months, the tables turned, and I had the incredible honor to serve her. *Thank God*, I did not have to report to a job. I didn't have to be anywhere for the most part. I had total time freedom. I was able to serve **her** and be there for **her**. During her last month, when she could barely walk, I carried her 75 pounds everywhere. I felt so honored to be her full time nurse. I found so much joy in serving her. That was a fulfilling experience that no price could ever be placed upon. I was able to put everything I had into serving her with dignity, grace, and tenderness as she had served me for 13 years prior.

6. SWEET SPOT FOR MY MARRIAGE– After Daisy was gone, that sweet spot in my heart that I had invested in her was so empty and saddened. I remember one night praying to God if I could just have 10 more minutes with her because I missed her so much! God was so faithful! I vividly recall having a dream with her in it! It was as if she was right there with me the whole time! I was so grateful that I was given those 10 more minutes. I just hugged her and played and snuggled with her the whole time. Daisy and I had this special communication with each other. We just knew what each other was saying. It's almost as if Daisy was telling me that the sweet spot I always had in my heart for her was now to transfer forward to Pete. I had placed Daisy so far ahead of anyone, including my husband, simply because she had required 24/7 attention with my complete care towards the end of her life. I did not spare one dime or one minute on her. Daisy was the lavished recipient of all my time and any money that I had. I gave it all to her in the ending months. My husband had gotten placed on the back burner for a little while. After she was gone, I actually did get to transfer that sweet spot in my heart forward to my marriage relationship. It has been a whole new level of sweetness in my marriage ever since.

CHAPTER 4

Maya from Brazil—
The Canine Latina Diva

In Dec of 2018, Maya found her way into our home all the way from Brazil through Dave and Yvette. I had no interest in having another dog so soon after Daisy's passing. Yvette had called two months prior, right after Daisy's passing, and shared that we had come to her mind as they were praying about what to do with this very special pup that they had rescued in Brazil. Almost two months later, after much thought and prayer, I felt peaceful to welcome Maya into our family. Yvette got Maya certified as an emotional support dog, and right away, they both were on the plane to Atlanta. It only took Maya a day or two, and she fit right in perfectly as if she already knew this was going to be her home all along. What a unique dog. Yvette was right! Maya is a human dog. It amazed me how many characteristics she has so similar to Daisy. I think what was more surprising is how quickly she mentally switched from **street dog** to **Canine Latina Diva**! She immediately assumed her throne in our home and remains completely clueless *(just as clueless as Daisy was)* that she is a dog. She loves bling, has unfiltered attitude, and loves to use her arms to hug and play constantly. Below, she is pictured hugging her older sister, Jade. She is also pictured with her rhinestone collar, leash and Christmas dress. She loves every bit of her bling! She's sexy and she knows it!

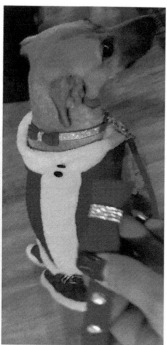

One day, we noticed Maya was dripping blood. What could be wrong with her? She was already spayed. We brought her to our holistic vet and found out she had developed a type of viral tumor and would need chemo. With my integrative health training, I was determined to find an alternative. It was a continual struggle as I continued to insist on *completely holistic* treatment. I gave her CBD hemp oil, raw food diet, along with several Chinese herbs and blends. I became frustrated as I saw very little progress. I finally surrendered my insistence on having her healed *my way*. I finally prayed, *"God, if you want her to have chemo, ok. I give up. I can't get anything to work."* I resolved to go with all the doctor's recommendations. I just didn't want to see my little princess bleed.

As soon as I finished that prayer, I looked to my side and saw a bottle of Oregano Essential Oil. The thought entered my mind about making her a homemade recipe of food. I thought, *turmeric for inflammation, oregano for viral, hemp seed for healing properties*. Then I researched the healthiest fruits and vegetables for canine consumption. My mind went into the zone. Literally, what seemed plucked out of thin air, I created this recipe for Maya:

My Dog Recipe:

1. Meat: Organic Farm raised, antibiotic & hormone free, free-range ground turkey or beef (alternate every 2 weeks).

2. Organic extra virgin coconut oil to cook the meat.

3. Spices: Tumeric, Essential Oregano Oil, Himalayan salt, Basil, Chia Seed, and Hemp Seed.

4. Vegetables/fruits: asparagus, brussels sprouts, green beans, sweet potatoes, pumpkin, cauliflower, spinach, carrots, blueberries, and apples.

The bleeding stopped. Thank God. I just needed to get out of my own way and allow God to inspire me instead. Maya is the greatest blessing bringing healing to everyone around her. Dawson especially connects with Maya. Maybe they relate to each other in some way as they've both found hope and love in their new home.

SECTION 5

Hope for Your Health and Wellness

CHAPTER 1

The Integrative Philosophy of Wellness

Living a lifestyle of health and wellness can be fun, enjoyable, and tremendously fulfilling. My health and wellness journey began in my early years as a child and has continued through my entire life. I was the child who was given a breakfast that consisted of an Instant Protein Drink, oatmeal, and 29 vitamins each day, while my schoolmates chugged down soda and fruit loops. I despised my parents for requiring us to live in a state of extreme health compared to my peers. My parents always threatened that if we didn't take all our vitamins and eat healthy, they would be stuck with this horrific doctor's bill! As a child, I believed the reasoning behind all the healthy eating was that it prevents scary doctor bills, when in essence, all my parents wanted to accomplish was keeping our bodies healthy.

It has always been a passion of mine to keep learning about health and all the science and research surrounding this popular subject. I received my certification as an Integrative Nutritional Health Coach from the Institute of Integrative Nutrition in New York. I've always appreciated the more functional integrative approach where health and wellness are viewed as a whole ecosystem connecting all of these following areas: spirituality, creativity, finances, career, education, health, physical activity, home cooking, home environment, relationships, social life, and joy. The areas are referenced in the IIN Circle of Life Diagram below on the left:

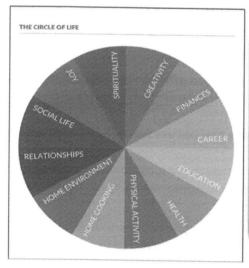

Each year, I write one or two goals in each of these areas to master on a vision board. I aim towards simplicity, balance, peace, and progress in each area, even if it is just a little bit.

Another way to unveil this concept is through the Integrative Nutrition Plate pictured above on the right. Nutrition is traditionally thought of as physical food that nourishes our body. However, according to an integrative health perspective, our PRIMARY FOOD is referred to as nourishment to our foundational needs which consist of: relationships, spirituality, physical activity, and career. Our SECONDARY FOOD is referred to as nourishment to our physical body which consists of fruits, vegetables, protein, whole grains, fats and oils, and water. It doesn't matter how healthy a food diet or "eating program" is considered, if the Primary Food area is not fed, then the Secondary Food area loses most of its value. For example, I discovered that if I ate perfect raw vegan for 2 weeks, but my relationships and spirituality were starved, the benefit from raw veganism was of minimal value. This entire approach made so much more sense to me.

This reformed pattern of thinking guided me from a traditional General Practitioner MD to an Integrative Functional Medicine MD. So far, this has been an enlightening experience. I had been taught most of my life to go to the doctor for sickness or disease treatment. A paradigm shift occurred in me when I had learned the value of going to the doctor to keep well so that I don't get sick in the first place. My functional medicine doctor reviews with me: my hormone levels, brain health, microbiome (gut health), toxicity levels, nutrition, and stress management. If that entire ecosystem in my body is optimally balanced, it is less likely I will experience sickness.

Unfortunately, this mindset is extremely dangerous to the life of Big Pharma, so it's not commonly taught in the mainstream. Think about it! Big Pharma would experience an economical crisis if we all became well! I've always taken responsibility for my own education and research as opposed to relying on the opinions of the mainstream. I never seemed to find much hope in conformity. Placing importance on my health and wellness has been instrumental to higher functioning in all areas of my life.

Even in my continual support of those recovering from addictions, integrative nutritional health can play an integral part of their overall success. I decided that if I was going to continue to help support those with addictions from a more integrative perspective, then it would be necessary to address addictions from a nutritional perspective in addition to a brain health perspective.

Dr. Daniel Amen is an internationally well-known double board-certified psychiatrist and best-selling author that uses SPECT imaging to determine levels of blood flow activity in the different areas of the brain. Dr. Amen has the largest research database of over 80,000 SPECT imaging scans pointing out patterns in the brain that evidence root causes of eating disorders, obesity, addiction, depression, anxiety, ADHD, PTSD, even marital conflict! I quickly learned that the diagnosis of the root causes of all health and wellness issues aren't just collected from inventories and symptom checklists. The root causes of these issues *originate* in the brain and can be best addressed by combining that collected information with looking *inside the brain* with imaging of the actual activity in the brain itself! I began to ask myself, could the root of most ailments and disease originate its roots in the brain? If so, then could we gain maximum health benefits through the mastery of our brain health? If the brain is the master control center of the entire body, could we learn to change our health by starting initially with the condition of the brain? These questions led me to receive my certification as an Amen Clinic Method Brain Health Coach.

Personally, after receiving the results of my own SPECT scanning, it was confirmed that I had Mild Traumatic Brain Injury and ADD. No wonder it seemed I had to work ten times harder than others to achieve significant results.

So the quest to become healthy was no longer an option, it has become a necessity in order to compensate and function at my highest potential.

(see pic below)

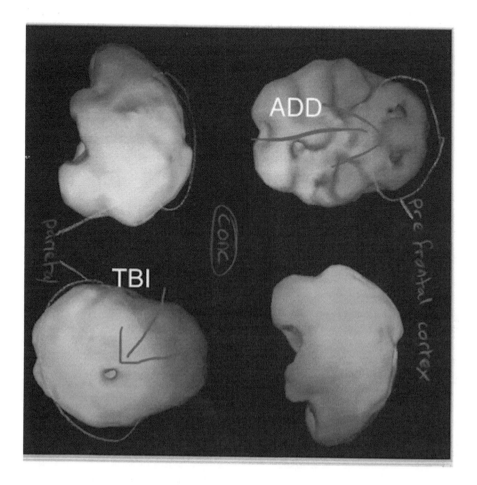

There are so many different diets and eating philosophies that have gone around society for years making it ludicrous to say that any one diet is the perfect one. All dietary theories have pros and cons. What may work well for one person, may not work well at all for another. Each person has individualized needs. However, universally, most experts would agree that if we all drank more water, ate more fruits and vegetables and whole foods, and reduced white sugar, white flour, and processed foods in our lives, and if we incorporated daily movement, we would all increase our health dramatically. Keep it simple. Find what works for you by a simple elimination diet and reintroduce one food at a time. Notice how your body reacts or feels to each food that is added back in. You will be the best judge about what works for you by the way you feel. There is hope for your health and wellness and your taste buds too!

CHAPTER 2

Hope for Your Taste Buds: Favorite Recipes

After completing my own SPECT brain imaging, my personal scans showed evidence of ADD (attention deficit disorder) and mild TBI (traumatic brain injury). Eating extremely healthy was no longer considered just a good habit for me, it became a necessity if I was to function optimally.

When my husband first met me in 2010, I drove him crazy as I would throw away any bread products he would purchase from the store—loaves of bread, hotdog buns, rolls, hamburger buns all in the garbage. The bread obsession actually started 20 years ago. Ever since my children were young, I milled my own organic grain and made my own flour which was used for all my bread and flour-based products. The only way that a grain of wheat could be healthy is to make sure it was GMO free (organic) and also to make sure that it had its 3 components (germ, gluten, and bran) still intact. There is not one bread product on a grocery store shelf that fulfills those requirements, hence all the recent gluten sensitivity occurrences. Go figure.

The wheat products in the store are mostly from GMO (genetically modified organisms), so it's no wonder all these sensitivities to gluten have arisen, our bodies cannot recognize this *altered* grain! Another problem with wheat flour-based products is that in order to have a shelf life, the germ and bran must be stripped out or else the product will go rancid. All that remains is the gluten. This creates a wheat flour product that is completely out of balance and unrecognizable by the body when 2 out of 3 of the necessary components have been removed. This produces what is called "wheat bread" on the shelves of the grocery store which is slightly brown and only has the gluten remaining. Guess what you get when you bleach the gluten? *White Bread.* You can learn all about the subject of healthful bread and flour products at Breadbeckers.com.

When I was first enlightened to this entire concept, my boys were only 2 and 3 years old. If I could choose only one healthy habit I could do for my family, it was going to be making my own homemade bread. No store-bought bread! My only problem was that I was in college with 2 young children and did not have two nickels to rub together. A grain mill at that time was a whopping $150 that I did not have. I prayed and made a promise to God that if He would provide that money for the mill, I would promise the rest of my days to make homemade bread and flour products, and to not ever feed my children bread from a grocery store shelf. The very next day, somebody accidentally bumped my car. My car was fine. We were fine. They gave me $150 for my inconvenience. ***Hot Slam Summer in the City!*** I went to Breadbeckers that very next day and purchased my grain mill.

I'm always cooking and creating healthful alternatives at home. My husband has told me for years that I should write a recipe book. Pete, this is the closest it will get for now to a recipe book. In this chapter, I'm going to include some healthy, yummy, easy foods and recipes that are some of my favorites. On the next few pages, you will find tasty *hopeful* recipes to promote brain health and optimal nutrition.

Homemade Bread made from Freshly Milled Grain:

(This recipe is from Breadbeckers Red Recipe book. We use this recipe with extreme moderation as we minimally consume bread. If we are going to consume bread, then you better believe it's this recipe.)

Throw the following ingredients into a bread machine. Bake in bread machine or take out after the dough cycle and form into your own shaped rolls, buns, or bread.

1. 1 ½ cups of warm/hot water *(not too hot, you'll kill the yeast)*

2. ½ cup of olive oil

3. ½ cup of honey

4. 2 tbsp. of sea salt

5. 1 organic egg

6. 4 ½ cups of freshly milled grain *(must use within a few hours to prevent from going rancid)*

7. 2 tbsp. of yeast

(3 loaves of hand-formed homemade bread)   (sandwich or burger buns)

Acai Bowl:

(This recipe is an amazing alternative to ice cream with all the "toppings." Get creative!)

1. In a blender, blend 1 packet of unsweetened açai *(found in frozen fruit section)* with ½ ripe banana, 1 cup of frozen blueberries *(or any mixed berry)*, and ¼ cup of coconut water until smooth.

2. Serve in a bowl and lavishly decorate with as many or as few optional toppings as you desire! *(e.g., Goji berries, coconut flakes, bee pollen, cacao nibs, chia seed, walnuts, or any other nuts, seeds, or fresh fruits.)*

Croccoli:

(This recipe is an ingenious tasty way to eat broccoli created and kid tested by my three nephews, Christian, Landon, and Spencer Banks.)

1. Steam Broccoli until bright green.

2. Sprinkle Coconut Aminos on the Broccoli.
   (Bragg's makes regular liquid aminos or liquid coconut aminos, found in most stores or on Amazon. It resembles soy sauce minus the sodium.)

3. Eat the flavorful *"croccoli"* and enjoy!

PB & J in a Bowl:

(This recipe is an alternative to the former obsession that my taste buds had to peanut butter and jelly.)

1. Place fresh organic blueberries and strawberries in a bowl.

2. Top with a nice big dollop of raw almond butter. *(I like crunchy!)*

3. Mix as you eat. Rare option: Sometimes I'll go a little crazy and add organic shredded coconut or bananas.

Soda and Pepperoni Chips (Movie Night):

(The "chips" in this recipe uses a dehydrator, an oven may be used as an alternative.)

Soda: Use your favorite brand of Sparkling Water (San Pellegrino, Perrier, etc.), add approximately ¼ dropperful of flavored liquid stevia to taste. *(My preference is to use Sweet Leaf Sweet Drops Liquid Stevia which can be purchased at Amazon or most grocery stores. We have all the flavors stocked in our refrigerator: Lemon, Cola, Grape, Valencia Orange, Vanilla Crème (tastes like cream soda), etc.*

Yummy all natural, clean, zero calorie soda!

Chips: Use 5 or 6 zucchinis. Peel. Slice in very thin discs. Place in a bowl with:

1. 1 tbsp. of Himalayan salt.

2. ¼ tbsp. of crushed red pepper flakes.

3. 1 tbsp. of garlic cloves.

Toss so that all the discs are coated, then cover, then let sit overnight. The salt will pull out the water. Drain the water the next day. Either spread on a cookie sheet and bake at 450 degrees Fahrenheit until crisp, or place in a dehydrator.

Chocolate Pudding: Avocado Chocolate Mousse

(This recipe is a DELICIOUS replacement for Chocolate Pudding)

1. Blend together in a Vita-Mix or blender:

    *   1 ripe avocado.

    *   1/3 cup of cacao powder.

    *   1/4 cup of raw local honey.

    *   1/4 cup of almond or coconut milk.

    *   1-2 tbsp. of vanilla extract.

2. Chill in refrigerator for minimum of 2-3 hours.

3. Serve it or serve sprinkled with shredded organic coconut and/or fresh banana slices.

Ants on a Log:

(This recipe is a super easy, yummy, fun, quick snack loaded with fiber.)

1. Wash fresh organic celery and cut each stalk into 4 pieces.

2. Fill with raw almond butter.

3. Top with Goji Berries or fresh blueberries.

Spaghetti Heaven:

(This recipe is an incredible replacement for Pasta! It can be a great all-veggie choice. You can never eat too many veggies!)

The Yellow Spaghetti Squash:

1. Take an entire yellow spaghetti squash whole and bake it in the oven for an hour *(go take a shower or work or do something else during that time—no need to wash it, just throw it in whole, straight from the store.)*

2. After an hour, remove from the oven. *(The insides will be soft making it simple to cut through.)* Cut longways with a long knife as pictured below.

3. Take a fork or spoon and scoop out all the seeds from the centers of the squash and discard.

4. Next, lightly sprinkle with olive oil and some Himalayan salt and pepper.

5. Place facing up into the oven and bake for another 15 minutes.

6. Remove from oven and use a clawed Spaghetti Server *(pictured below)* to scoop out all the squash. It will look just like spaghetti. It should easily come right out.

During that 15 minutes, you can quickly whip together a quick marinara sauce.

The Marinara Quick Sauce: *(just like my grandma taught me)*

1. In a medium saucepan, place desired amount of organic extra virgin olive oil and heat on medium. Do not exceed medium heat.

2. Sprinkle into the oil any of the following spices in whatever amount desired:

(Spices must infuse in warm oil to pull out their true essence. Try to make them organic to avoid ingesting pesticides that non-organic spices are heavily sprayed with. You can add or delete anything, get creative here):

- Oregano

- Basil

- Rosemary

- Thyme

- Small dash of red pepper

- Garlic

- Himalayan salt & pepper

3. Add in 3 cans of organic diced tomatoes and 1 can of tomato paste to the oil and spice mixture. Add water as desired for consistency.

4. Stir, then taste to see if your spices are right so you can adjust if needed. You may want to add a bit more salt to achieve the desired flavor. Some add parmesan.

5. If you prefer smooth sauce over chunky, then blend your sauce in the blender.

You can optionally add meat to this sauce if desired.

To make a healthy meat option:

1. Brown Organic Ground Turkey in a pan.

2. Add in these ***magic*** four to achieve a "sausage flavor:" salt, pepper, rosemary, and thyme.

When serving all of this together, you can add parmesan to the top just like spaghetti, some choose to use nutritional yeast flakes as an alternative to parmesan.

Conclusion

There is *hope* for restoration, healing, and magnificent completeness in all of our lives that is intended to take place when you have a full connection with God without blockages. My prayer for you is that you find *hope* in every area of your life and realize that there is *hope* available to reach your greatest potential. There is *hope* for finding your purposes and passions and you will experience freedom to create liberally according to those purposes and passions. Hope is always there for you, through the discovery of your calling, your struggles, your breakthroughs, and with the community of believers.

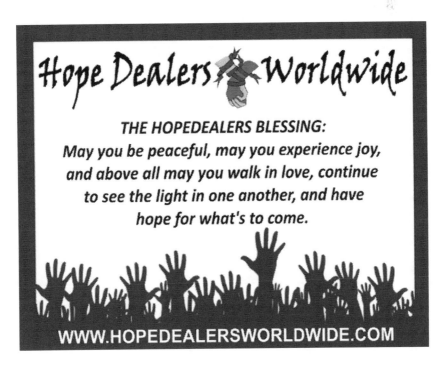

Next Steps

Now that you have perused through the endless stories of hope, you may be wondering, what's next? How can I help with the Hopedealers Worldwide movement?

Hopedealers Worldwide, Inc. is a registered 501c3 organization. You can view our website at www.hopedealersworldwide.com for more information on the services that we offer. At the time of the writing of this book, Hopedealers Worldwide currently serves the community and also those whose lives have been touched by the disease of addiction by offering:

1. CADC (Certified Alcohol and Drug Counselor) Certification Classes. (scholarships available).

2. Free assistance with application and enrollment for Marketplace Health Insurance.

3. Adventure Therapeutic Travel Experiences and/or Service Projects.

4. Community Groups & Classes.

5. Substance Abuse Evaluations/Assessments & Individual/Group Counseling.

6. Domestic Violence Evaluations/Assessments & Individual/Group Counseling.

7. Anger Management Evaluations/Assessments & Individual/Group Counseling.

8. Brain Health Assessments & Coaching (Amen Clinic Method).

9. Integrative Nutritional & Lifestyle Health Coaching.

Your contribution or participation in any of the above services supports the recovery of those who are committed to a drug-free future and lifestyle. You can help make a difference. Visit www.hopedealersworldwide.com to make a donation or learn more about our services offered. Nadine is also available for speaking engagements, phone, or video consultation.

ACKNOWLEDGMENTS

Mom and Dad, Nick and Dianne Blase, if you did not create me and encourage me to learn so many of the qualities and disciplines I have this far, then I wouldn't even be here. This book certainly would have never been written. You have been the foundation for my faith, and I would not be who I am today without your example.

My husband Pete, for supporting and facilitating many of the experiences that have occurred in my life without blockage and for putting up with me through many of my journeys, lessons, and expenses.

My older sister, Nicole Blase Arnold, (on the right) for always knowing best and always being right, for being my fashion police in the 80s, my design expert, social coach, and in all areas, you just know what's right and you stick to it. Also, I'm inspired by your devotion and faithfulness to what is honorable and Godly and moral and for your inspiration of being an innovative, creative, effective, and successful entrepreneur and a fantastic mom.

My younger sister, Noelle Blase Banks, (on the left) who has a heart of gold. You are a fantastic mommy of all your 2 legged and 4 legged children. You inspire me the way you strive for excellence in all areas above and beyond. So thankful that you are a breast cancer champion survivor, and you are always there. You are always giving to those less fortunate and treat others with the highest respect.

I also want to extend thanks and gratitude to several of my family and friends that are too many to mention here. But I will try! Thank you to those who have offered tremendous support in various ways. Many of you have dealt hope to me and have dealt hope with me that *I have not already* mentioned in previous chapters.

**Thanks to all in my family community
that I have not mentioned previous chapters:**

Helen Psareas, Margaret Blase Cohen and David Cohen, Scott Porter, Carol LaFache, Brad Banks, Larry and Carol Chkoreff, Tiffany Mason, Brian Arnold, Tyler Arnold, Paul Psareas, Phil and Jess Psareas, Gina Psareas Finney, Rosemary Pascucci, David Pascucci, Barb & Rick Pascucci, Rick Pascucci III, Maria Pascucci-Maciejewski, Joanne & Rocco Laurienzo, John and Jen Blase, Rosemary Sperber Blase, Greg Blase, Gretchen Blase Kreidler, Eric Kreidler, Kara LaFache, Trisha LaFache, John Wade, Mark Wade, and James Kalra.

In remembrance with loving thoughts and respects
to my family members who are no longer with us.
Each one inspired me in their own special ways:

Grandpa Nicholas Blase Sr. (1916-1974)

Grandma Margaret Mary Coletta Blase (1915-2012)

Uncle Richie Pascucci (1931-2002)

Aunt Maria Blase Wade (1942-2003)

Uncle Mike Violante (1916-2006)

Aunt Laura Violante (1922-2009)

Uncle John Blase Sr. (1943-2009)

Thanks to my friends in my travel and personal growth & development community that I have not mentioned in previous chapters. I am deeply grateful for your friendships and for the culture we've co-created. You are family to me. You have all helped me rewrite my story . . . which writes WV's story.

Nathan and Mindy Blair, Daniel and Vanessa Rotoni, Jamie & Venus Parker, Vince Paul, Erwin & Diana Mendoza, Tarid Powell, Donald and Fran Ely, Doug Loyd, James Passmore, Lyn Barger, Randy Hudson, Becky Vargas, Arturo and Stephanie Ruiz, Miguel Zapata, Gustavo Velasco, Armando Negrete, Aida Juarez Hernandez, Pedro Flores, Jennifer Collie, Mama Terrie Bardwell, Sherry Baer, John Webster, Colette West, Marsha Ellis, Jay and Ashley Nelson, Ingrid Meiners, James and Victoria Hightower, Tom and Betty Phillips, Jeff and Paula Berlier, Chris and Rhonda Breaux, Lydia Nugent, Rhonda Morris, Kelly Accetta, Lisa and Michael Head, David Cox, Mike Marich, Keith Brown, Mark Accetta, Mama Gail Spears, Julian Bernard, Jerome Fitts, Mama Dot Norman, Antavius DJ Tay, Willie Myers, Camitzy and Jared Ojeda, Terri Mabry, April Pullins, Rich & Janelle Isip, Tere and Mary Kampe, Susan Schrag, Ann Kesselman, Marri Glass, Robert & Cathy Casteel, Michael and Katie Catlow, Lorenzo Roybal, Brian and Sarah Brown, Roscoe Taylor, Joshua Wilson, Lynn Mantanona, Alison Dealy, Austin Wright, Denise Etzel, Valerie Finley, Lisa Michaels, Judy Keating, Chanelle Johnston, Shelly Anderson, Cindy Lopez, Tammie Ellis, Jen Clarke, Ana and Nestor Diaz, Randy and Sharon Kline, Hollie Hart, Angie Cuff, Rudy and Salina Atilano, Suzanne Schaefer, Shirley and Freddie Keys, Cheryl Shalhout, Beverly Hyacinth, Darlene Martin, Micheal and Abby Donaldson, Cesar and Pamela Ruiz, Eric Happy Gusevik, Deb Carmody, Mike Madren, and Davide Di Giorgio, Hollis Colbert, Roy Woods, Roberta Barcena, Justin Call, Eddie Head, Amy Wake Varley, Johnny Wimbrey, Johnnie Vivirito, Janie and Raymond Braun, Adam Flores, and Larri Rose, and Srinivas Bhat.

Thanks to all our family friends.
We are grateful for your friendships.

Valerie Hall, Josh Perez, Ralph and Loryn Walker, Glenn and Lisa Carver, Bonnie Silverman, Bill Neglia, Ralston Medouze, Nancy Wells, Sindy Marvin, Tyler Johnson, Greg Griffin, David Clarke, Janie Montague, Chris Rechter, Lee Ann Sherry, Tracy Moore, Ann Lafferty, Courtney Epps, Charlene Hicks, Patrick Thomas, Cynthia Samuels, Seth Benator, Tracy Lefabre, Tibby Mangrum, Larry Cole, Giselle Williams, Shari Wessler, Karen Vining, Katie Warechowski, Aurea McGarry, C. Nicole Henderson, Carolyn Lacy, Margaret Waage, and Jean Rogers, Tommy and Brandi Stevenson, Sherri Jessie, Michael Kennedy, Katy McCormick, and Carolyn Polakowski.

Ruth Fuller, Jay & Christy Wall, Robin Rayne Nelson, Kathy Taylor, Jennifer Hughes, Nancy Trott, Sylvia Venable, Paul Wilson, Russell & Pam Rice, Rob and Lorraine Kenny, Keith and Phyllis Rife, Pat Stells, John & Lisa Thomas, Meli Neal, Nancy Kraft, Leanne Maranto Hooper, Fay and Carter Harbin, Courtney Marks, Katie Chandler, Barbara Morgan, Nicole Shuey, Tony & Jessica Reynolds, Matt Scott, Anthony Panzica, Linda Panzica, Charity Holman, Tyrone Hawkins, Chris Elder, Hannah Smith, Rob & Michelle Smith, Amanda Redwine, Robert Greene, Teisha Ault, Tina Moore, Ginger Floyd, Cindy Hix, Dena Voyles-Padgett, Jason Ortiz, Mary Rogers, Tony Cole, James Hatfield, Michelle Neese, Heather Greco, Natalie Kelly, Dave Rogers, Jason Pittman, Daniel Pollard, Lynne Saunders, and John & Jessie Hutchins.

ABOUT THE AUTHOR

Nadine Blase Psareas, a native of Utica, New York, has been a resident of Atlanta, Georgia since 1985. She is a graduate of Lassiter High School in Marietta, Georgia, and received her BSED degree at the University of Georgia. She served as an elementary school teacher for ten years in Georgia before early retirement. Having experienced at age 19 a mission trip to Haiti that redirected her path in life, Nadine studied to become a teacher and inner healing counselor. She is also a Certified Anger Management Specialist, Domestic Violence Specialist, an Integrative Nutrition Health Coach, and also a Certified Brain Health Coach through the Amen Clinics. She is currently completing her CADC II (Certified Alcohol and Drug Counselor). Now as a Global Organization Leader for a pace-setting travel and lifestyle corporation, Nadine identified a unique opportunity to combine travel with a concept her company created "Voluntourism" using travel to underserved communities as an opportunity to fortify the success of young drug addiction victims to have long-term success in recovery through giving to those in dire straights more powerful than those struggling with addiction could comprehend. She is now the founder of a 501c3 organization, Hopedealers Worldwide, that supports others whose lives are touched by the disease of addiction. She enjoys yoga, outdoor activities, wellness and nutrition, and of course, creating memories and collecting smiles with her husband, children, and family dogs. In addition to being a mother of six, in 2017, she welcomed into her home and became the guardian of a special needs young man in the community whose parents are both deceased. In 2018, Nadine was the recipient of the first ever "Rudy" Award, given by football legend, Rudy Ruettiger and nominated by her peers and community for exemplifying the 4 "C"'s (character, commitment, contribution, and courage). Just before the release of this book, Nadine received the honor of being selected as a Legacy Award Nominee at Aurea McGarry's Live Your Legacy Summit for her dedication to helping people suffering from addiction and supporting their families in the process.

THANK YOU FOR READING MY BOOK!

Please leave me a review on Amazon!

Thanks so much!
Nadine Blase Psareas

Made in the USA
Columbia, SC
29 January 2024

30668949R00120